An Unauthorized Biography

Andy Warhol

"Everyone Will be Famous for 15 Minutes"

Read about other

American REBELS

James Dean
*"Dream As If You'll
Live Forever"*
0-7660-2537-3

Kurt Cobain
*"Oh Well, Whatever,
Nevermind"*
0-7660-2426-1

Jimi Hendrix
"Kiss The Sky"
0-7660-2449-0

Madonna
"Express Yourself"
0-7660-2442-3

American REBELS

An Unauthorized Biography

Andy Warhol

"Everyone Will be Famous for 15 Minutes"

Edward Willett

Enslow Publishers, Inc.
40 Industrial Road
Box 398
Berkeley Heights, NJ 07922
USA

http://www.enslow.com

Library of Congress Cataloging-in-Publication Data

Willett, Edward, 1959-
  Andy Warhol : "everyone will be famous for 15 minutes" / Edward Willett.
      p. cm. — (American rebels)
  Includes bibliographical references and index.
  Summary: "A biography of avant-garde painter, printmaker, and filmmaker Andy Warhol, discussing his early struggles, rise to fame as a controversial pop artist, personal hardships, and legacy"—Provided by publisher.
  ISBN 978-0-7660-3385-6
  1. Warhol, Andy, 1928-1987—Juvenile literature. 2. Artists—United States—Biography—Juvenile literature. I. Warhol, Andy, 1928-1987. II. Title. III. Title: Everyone will be famous for 15 minutes.
  N6537.W28W58 2010
  700.92—dc22
  [B]
                                            2009017596

Printed in the United States of America

042010 Lake Book Manufacturing, Inc., Melrose Park, IL

10 9 8 7 6 5 4 3 2 1

To Our Readers:
This book has not been authorized by Andy Warhol's estate or its successors. We have done our best to make sure all Internet Addresses in this book were active and appropriate when we went to press. However, the author and the publisher have no control over and assume no liability for the material available on those Internet sites or on other Web sites they may link to. Any comments or suggestions can be sent by e-mail to comments@enslow.com or to the address on the back cover. Every effort has been made to locate all copyright holders of material used in this book. If any errors or omissions have occurred, corrections will be made in future editions of this book.

✿ Enslow Publishers, Inc., is committed to printing our books on recycled paper. The paper in every book contains 10% to 30% post-consumer waste (PCW). The cover board on the outside of each book contains 100% PCW. Our goal is to do our part to help young people and the environment too!

Illustration Credits: Miloš Adame, p. 13; Associated Press, pp. 9, 17, 109, 120, 134; Image used courtesy of Carnegie Mellon University Archives, p. 31; Photographs of artists taken by Dena, Archives of American Art, Smithsonian Institution. p. 95; Ellen Hulda Johnson papers, Archives of American Art, Smithsonian Institution, p. 6; Everett Collection, p. 101; Nils Jorgensen/Rex USA/Courtesy Everett Collection, p. 125; Managing editor Russell Lynes' artists' files, Archives of American Art/Smithsonian Institution, p. 38; Fred W. McDarrah/Getty Images, pp. 57, 62, 67; Mirrorpix/Courtesy of Everett Collection, p. 71; © Orion/Courtesy Everett Collection, p. 92; Photofest, p. 82; Time & Life Pictures/Getty Images, p. 45; Felipe Trueba/Photoshot/Landov, p. 51.

Cover Illustration: Getty Images Entertainment/Getty Images.

Contents

Andy Warhol in 1963 in front of one of his paintings.

Introduction

On July 9, 1962, an unusual art exhibition opened in the Ferus Gallery in Los Angeles. It consisted of thirty-two paintings of Campbell's Soup cans—one painting for each flavor of soup the company offered—wrapped around the gallery on a narrow white shelf, very much as if they were real cans on display in a supermarket.

The gallery owner, Irving Blum, didn't do much to advertise. He simply sent out a postcard of a tomato-soup can inviting interested buyers to stop by. There was no official opening. The paintings, measuring twenty by sixteen inches each, were priced at one hundred dollars each.

Visitors to the gallery were "extremely mystified," Blum said later. Another gallery not too far away bought dozens of real Campbell's Soup cans, put them in the window, and offered to sell them cheaper: just sixty cents for three cans. "There was a lot of hilarity concerning them," he noted, but no serious interest from collectors. Actor Dennis Hopper bought one, but in all only six paintings were sold.[1]

Despite the lack of buyers, the paintings attracted a lot of publicity—both good and bad. Critics and gallery visitors alike either loved them or loathed them.

The publicity began two months earlier in a *Time* magazine article published May 11, 1962: "It was said of Zeuxis, the great artist of ancient Greece, that he could paint a bunch of grapes so realistically that birds would try to eat them. This was an impressive skill, but art has long since aspired to more than carbon-copy realism."

But "a segment of the advance guard," a group of painters unknown to each other, the *Time* article went on, "has suddenly pulled a switch," coming to the conclusion that "the most banal and even vulgar trappings of modern civilization can, when transposed literally to canvas, become Art."

Among the painters briefly mentioned in the *Time* article was a thirty-year-old New York-based commercial artist named Andy Warhol, who "is currently occupied with a series of 'portraits' of Campbell's Soup Cans in living color."

"I just paint things I always thought were beautiful, things you use every day and never think about," Warhol told *Time*. "I just do it because I like it."[2]

The *Time* article was entitled "The Slice-of Cake School," but a new name, Pop Art, was already taking hold. Within a few years, Warhol had become the Prince of Pop, the most famous creator of this new style of art, so different from what had come before.

Warhol's Campbell's soup cans were displayed at the Museum of Modern Art in 2002.

Eventually the Pop Art movement ended, but Warhol's fame continued. For the last twenty-five years of his life, he was one of the most famous and recognizable people in the world. However, he wasn't necessarily one of the most popular. Controversy constantly swirled around him. People loathed him or loved him, applauded him or reviled him. Some swung from one extreme to the other: one former associate and admirer even tried to kill him.

"In the future everybody will be world-famous for 15 minutes," Warhol once famously said.[3] But his own fame lasted a lot longer than that. Indeed, he's as famous—and as controversial—now as he was when he died more than twenty years ago, with new exhibitions of his work mounted on a regular basis around the world.

Those Campbell's Soup can paintings? Irving Blum bought them back from Dennis Hopper and the few other buyers, then purchased the entire set from Warhol for one thousand dollars. In 1996, the Museum of Modern Art acquired them from Blum for an estimated $15 million.[4] Warhol would have loved that.

A trendsetter rather than a trend-follower, a dispassionate observer of both the seamy and celebrity sides of life, Warhol was a true American rebel. And in true American fashion, his life started in very humble circumstances.

Chapter 1

Early Days

Andy Warhol told a lot of stories about his childhood after he was famous. He'd talk about having to eat soup made with tomato ketchup while growing up in the Depression. He talked about his father being a coal miner who died when he was young, and whom he hardly saw. He said his brothers bullied him, that his mother was always sick, that nobody liked him, that he never had any friends, that his skin turned white and his hair fell out by the time he was twelve.[1]

A lot of the stories weren't true. But Andy Warhol was never someone to let truth get in the way of a good story—especially about himself.

Born in Pittsburgh

Andy Warhol was born Andrew Warhola on August 6, 1928, in his parents' bedroom in a narrow red-brick house in Pittsburgh, Pennsylvania. He had two older brothers, Paul, born on June 26, 1922, and John, born on May 31, 1925.

His parents, Ondrej and Julia Warhola, were recent immigrants from the Ruthenian village of Mikova, located in the Carpathian Mountains (known in popular culture as the home of the vampire Dracula) near the borders of Russia and Poland.

Ondrej was born in Mikova on November 28, 1889. The Warhola family were devout, hardworking people, and Ondrej grew up working in the fields. When he was seventeen he decided there was no future in his homeland and he emigrated to Pittsburgh. After working there for two years, he went back to Mikova to find a bride.

He found Julia Zavacky, born in Mikova on November 17, 1892, one of a family of fifteen children (though only nine survived until Julia was in her teens). Her brothers, John and Andrew, had already moved to Pennsylvania. According to Warhol biographer Victor Bockris, who interviewed family members extensively for his book *Warhol*, Julia and her sister Mary wanted to be famous singers, and even sang with a gypsy caravan in the Mikova area for a season. Julia was also artistic, making small sculptures and painting designs on objects. When she was sixteen her father told her it was time for her to get married. When Ondrej Warhola, who had just been the best man at the Pennsylvania wedding of Julia's brother, John, returned and wanted to marry her, she at first refused; but her father beat her and then asked the priest to tell her to marry him. "Andy (Ondrej) visits again. He brings candy, wonderful candy. And for this candy, I marry him," she used to say.[2] The couple lived in Mikova for three years, then Ondrej went back to Pittsburgh to avoid being drafted into the army of Emperor Franz Joseph to fight in the First Balkan War. The couple didn't see each other again for nine years.

Julia was pregnant when Ondrej left, and gave birth in 1913. The baby girl died of influenza when she was just six weeks old. Not long after that Julia heard that her brother Yurko had been killed in the war. It later turned out the news was a mistake, but the shock may have contributed to the death of Julia's mother, just a month later. That left Julia to look after her little sisters, Ella and Eva, who were then six and nine.

A statue of Andy Warhol stands outside a museum dedicated to him in Slovakia.

Things went from bad to worse. The First World War broke out. The area was ravaged, and Julia's house was burned down. Ondrej's brother George was killed. Several times she had to hide out in the woods with her little sisters to escape approaching soldiers.

When the war ended, Ondrej began trying to bring Julia to the United States. In 1919, he tried five times to send her the fare, but none of the money reached her. In 1921, she finally took matters into her own hands. Just before the United States embargoed immigration from Eastern Europe, Julia borrowed $180 from a priest and used it to travel by wagon, train, and finally ship to find her husband in Pittsburgh.

By the time Andy was born, Ondrej, then thirty-eight years old, was a bald, muscular man who worked twelve hours a day for the Eichleay Corporation, a company that built roads and moved houses (not the contents of the houses but the houses themselves, to make way for new construction). Although he didn't work in a coal mine, as Andy sometimes claimed, it was true that he was often away, called to work out of town for weeks or months.

Julia, thirty-five, had not been assimilated into American life as well as her husband. She still couldn't speak a word of English. She typically wore a long peasant dress under an apron, and covered her head with a babushka. Both Julia and Ondrej were devout Byzantine Catholics who walked their family six miles to mass every Sunday morning.

14

The Depression Hits Home

In 1930, the Warhola family moved into a larger house. Julia's sister Mary lived nearby. Two other brothers and another sister lived not too far away, and Ondrej's brother Joseph also lived in the neighborhood. Between them and their families, little Andek (as Andy's mother called him) grew up surrounded by relatives.

As the Great Depression took hold, the family suffered economically. Ondrej lost his job. Fortunately, he had managed to save several thousand dollars from his earnings during the 1920s. Now he had to rely on those savings to feed his family. The Warholas were comparatively lucky. On January 16, 1931, relief organizations in Pittsburgh noted that 47,750 people were at starvation level in the city.[3]

The Warholas moved again, into a two-room apartment on Moultrie Street, where all three boys had to sleep in the same bed. The crowded conditions probably contributed to tensions between Paul and John, who often fought. Julia began working part-time, cleaning houses and windows. She also made flower sculptures out of tin cans. Paul sold newspapers on streetcars for nickels and dimes.

When Andy was four years old, his father regained his job with the Eichleay Corporation and was once again called away on jobs, leaving Paul, then ten years old, as head of the household. Paul was having problems at school. He hadn't been able to speak English when he started first grade, and as a result he hated public speaking, a problem which became worse when he developed a speech impediment. He began to skip school, and took out some of his frustrations by disciplining his littlest brother.

Andy apparently needed some discipline, though his big brother probably wasn't the best person to administer it. "You could see he was picking up things much better than we had, but he was mischieful [sic] between the ages of three to six," Paul explained later about Andy picking up bad language from kids in the street and using it around his relatives. "The more you smacked him, the more he said it, the worse he got."[4]

In September 1932, when Andy had just turned four, Paul decided he should be registered for school. But the first day went badly—a girl slapped him, and he was almost two years younger than the other students—and Julia told Paul not to force him to go back. For the next two years, while Paul and John were in school, Andy was alone with his mother.

Julia was very creative. Not only did she draw pictures, she also loved embroidery—fabrics she'd embroidered decorated their home—and enjoyed making beautifully decorated Easter eggs.[5] When she was alone with Andy, she would draw pictures with him: portraits of each other or pictures of the cat.

New Neighborhood, New Friends

In early 1934, the Warhola family moved again, this time into a house in the Oakland neighborhood of Pittsburgh. Ondrej paid $3,200 for the two-story brick house, which was much nicer than anything else the family had lived in up to that point. Andy would live

The Warhola's Pittsburgh home, in the Oakland section, seen here in 2005.

there until he moved to New York in 1949. He and John shared a bedroom; Paul converted the attic into a third bedroom for himself. There were lots of boys around, playing horseshoes, softball or baseball, swimming in Schenley Park, and playing craps. But, remembers a neighbor, "Andy was so intelligent, he was more or less in a world all of his own, he kept to himself like a loner."[6]

When Andy did play with other children, he usually preferred to play with girls. His first best friend at Holmes Elementary School, located just half a block from the Warholas' new house, was a little Ukrainian girl named Margie Girman. They'd go to the movies together on Saturday mornings. At the theater, for just eleven cents, children got an ice-cream bar, a double feature, and a signed eight-by-ten glossy photograph of one of the movie's stars. Andy collected them and soon had a whole box of them.

When Julia would take her children to visit her family in Lyndora, Pennsylvania, Andy's best friend was Lillian "Kiki" Lanchester. When they went to visit Julia's sister Mary, Andy's best friend was his cousin Justina, nicknamed Tinka. She was four years older than Andy and like a big sister to him.

Though Andy had only been at Soho Elementary in their old neighborhood for one day when he was four, he was credited with having completed the first grade there, and so he went straight into Grade 2 at Holmes Elementary, at the age of six. Even then, his teacher, Catherine Metz, remembered later, "he was real good at drawing."[7]

Andy liked school and did well—and all the time he was drawing. Julia encouraged him, even buying a movie projector (without her husband's knowledge) so he could watch black-and-white silent cartoons, which inspired him to draw even more.

Andy had a number of health problems as he grew up. When he was two, his eyes would swell up and had to be washed out with boric acid solution every day. When he was four he broke his right arm after tripping over the streetcar tracks. Nobody realized it was broken until it had healed crooked: the doctors had to rebreak the bone so it could heal straight. When he was six he had scarlet fever. When he was seven he had his tonsils removed.

In the autumn of 1936, when he was eight years old, he came down with rheumatic fever.

Eight Weeks in Bed

Now, rheumatic fever is rare in the United States, although outbreaks are still common in the developing world. It's a complication of strep throat in which the bacteria that cause the strep infection move into the rest of the body, producing inflammation that can damage the heart, joints, skin, and brain.

If the brain is affected, the inflammation can cause loss of coordination and uncontrolled movement of the limbs and face. Technically this is called chorea, but a more common name for it is St. Vitus' dance. In the 1930s, doctors weren't sure what caused it, but they did know that it usually disappeared on its own within weeks or months.

Teachers at Holmes Elementary had already discovered Andy's artistic talent, but now he found when he tried to draw on the blackboard his hand would begin to shake. He had trouble writing his name or tying his shoes. Kids laughed at him and began to pick on him and beat him up. Suddenly, school became a terrifying place.

His family didn't notice the symptoms at first, but once he started having trouble talking and sitting still, and began fumbling things, they finally called the doctor. He ordered Andy to stay in bed for a month.

Andy loved it. He had his mother all to himself, and didn't have to deal with the bullies at school or his brothers or father. His mother gave him movie magazines and comic books and coloring books and moved the radio into the dining room, where his bed had been moved. Once his hands stopped shaking, Andy spent hours coloring, making collages with cut-up magazines, and playing with paper dolls.

After four weeks he was supposed to go back to school, but he suffered a relapse and had to go back to bed for another four weeks. After the second four weeks, he'd developed one of the other possible complications of rheumatic fever: large reddish-brown patches on his skin.

In addition to blotches, rheumatic fever can cause lumps or nodules to appear beneath normal-appearing skin. Skin problems would plague Andy for the rest of his life.

Those eight weeks in bed proved to be important for Andy Warhol's artistic development. In the movie magazines and through the radio, he immersed himself in a rich fantasy world, one filled with celebrities and focused on the two centers of American popular culture: Hollywood and New York. His most prized possession for years was a personalized signed photograph of the child star Shirley Temple. He went so far as to emulate many of the actress's gestures, carrying them on into adult life. His fascination with celebrities would be a driving force for much of his career.

Those eight weeks also contributed a great deal to the development of his personality. Back in school, the bullying slacked off. Andy was now seen as slightly eccentric and somewhat frail. His brothers began standing up for him more. He played on all of that to his benefit.

Many years later, Warhol wrote, "I learned when I was little that whenever I got aggressive and tried to tell someone what to do, nothing happened—I just couldn't carry it off. I learned that you actually have more power when you shut up, because at least that way people will start to maybe doubt themselves."[8]

Or as Victor Bockris puts it, "His two-sided character began to emerge. While continuing to be as sweet and humble as ever with his girlfriends, he began on occasion to act like an arrogant little prince at home."[9]

That home was soon to undergo another major upheaval, with the death of Andy's father.

The Start of the Art

The health of Andy's father slowly failed over the years. By the end of the 1930s, Ondrej was still working twelve hours a day, six days a week. Then he travelled to a job in Wheeling, West Virginia. He and several other men there drank contaminated water. When he returned home, he became so ill with jaundice (a yellowing of the skin caused by a malfunctioning liver, the organ that filters contaminants from the blood) that he was confined to bed and unable to work. To make extra money, the family took in boarders. As a result, the now older Paul and John began to spend more and more time away from home. Paul had dropped out of high school and began working in a steel mill, and he had taken up gambling. Ondrej didn't trust him to look after the family finances after he was gone, and so began to tell relatives to listen to John when it came to financial matters. This made the long-simmering conflict between Paul and John worse. The bickering and tension in the home must have strongly affected Andy, who was only eleven when his father fell ill.

Andy was fourteen when his father went into the hospital for a series of tests and never came out. Five days after entering the hospital, Ondrej Warhola died. In keeping with cultural tradition, the body was laid out in the house for three days, with someone keeping vigil every night. Andy refused to look at the body: in fact, he hid under his bed.[1] For the rest of his life he had such a fear of death that his father's funeral was probably the only one he ever attended.

Paul married in 1943. He and his wife, Ann, moved into the second floor of the house. Ann and Andy did not get along. Neither, it turned out, did Paul and Ann. The house became something of a battleground. The situation was made even worse when Paul was drafted and joined the United States Navy, leaving his pregnant wife in Julia's care. But Julia, who had always been strong and resilient, fell ill. Ann, to everyone's relief, moved back with her own parents.

Julia's doctor diagnosed colon cancer, and performed a colostomy, an operation in which the entire bowel system is removed. The operation was successful, though Julia later doubted whether she had had cancer at all. Julia recovered remarkably well, but the experience was traumatic for Andy, who adored his mother and had lost his father only two years earlier. Now, along with his fear of funerals, he developed a horror of hospitals and surgeons that may even have contributed to his death.

Andy's First Art Lessons

But through all of this upheaval, Andy had one thing he loved and could always turn to: his art. Although Pittsburgh was a smoky, dirty steel town, it was actually a great place to study art. Not only did the public schools specialize in teaching it, but Pittsburgh was home to three extremely wealthy, art-collecting families, the Carnegies, the Mellons, and the Fricks. Their interest in art led them to sponsor art competitions, art centers, and free Saturday-morning art classes for talented children at the Carnegie Museum.

In 1937, when he was nine, Andy Warhola was recommended for the Carnegie Museum course by his Holmes Elementary School art teacher, Annie Vickermann. Students had to be recommended by their teachers, but the art supplies were free.

Students in grades 5 to 7 were known as the Tam O'Shanters. Students in grades 8 to 10 were known as the Palettes. There were so many art students on Saturday mornings that it took half an hour just for them to enter the building, gather their materials, and find a seat in the Music Hall, where the classes were taught.

"The Tam O'Shanters . . . started early Saturday morning, and no transportation or lunch was provided, and no lollipops were handed out," recalled Andy's teacher, James Fitzpatrick, in a 1987 interview. "I would tell the youngsters that when you come here, you come to learn. That's what your parents expect."[2]

And learn Andy did. The course was designed to give students a good background so they could pursue any kind of career in art. Local artists sometimes dropped by and talked about their work. Sometimes the children visited exhibitions in the museum. And always they drew.

Fitzpatrick immediately saw something unique in Andy. "He was so individualistic and ahead of his time," he said. "He was magnificently talented."

But if Fitzpatrick caught a glimpse of what was to come in Andy's career, he also caught a glimpse of what was to come in his personal life, adding that Andy was also "a little bit obnoxious. He had no consideration for other people. . . . He was socially inept. . . . He was not pleasant."[3]

High School Days

In September 1941, during his father's long period as an invalid, Andy began attending Schenley High School, a twenty-minute walk from his house. He had become a teenager just at the time when the very concept of "teenager" first began to emerge, along with the first distinct popular culture for teens: bobby sox, saddle shoes, jitterbugging, and the first idol to cause teenaged girls to swoon and scream: Frank Sinatra. Andy was a serious student. He drew almost constantly, his artwork piling up around the house to the point his mother once dumped a bunch of it into the trash. "He wasn't part of any of the cliques, he was sort of left out, but he wasn't in the art club because his talent was so superior to the rest of us," remembered Lee Karageorge, a classmate of Andy's in his freshman and sophomore years.[4]

In his junior and senior years, one of Andy's teachers was none other than James Fitzpatrick, who had taught the Saturday morning classes at the Carnegie Museum. He pushed Andy to do more than he thought he could do.

As had been true earlier in his childhood, most of Andy's friends in high school were girls. He was still friends with Margie Girman, whose friend Mirna Serbin recalled later that "Andy was different than the other boys—he wasn't tough or frightening, and he didn't want to do anything wrong with you."[5]

Aside from his art classes, the greatest influence on Andy during high school was probably the movies, the single greatest form of popular culture of the 1940s. Radio was close behind. He also read lots of magazines and newspapers, and was particularly attracted to their photographs, which he cut out and used in collages and drawings.

Like many teenagers before and since, Andy felt he was missing out on more exciting things that were happening elsewhere. "You can only live life in one place at a time," he wrote in his book *America*, but "you live in your dream America that you've custom-made from art and schmaltz and emotions just as much as you live in your real one."[6]

Throughout his high school years, Andy looked forward to college. He was accepted by both the University of Pittsburgh and the Carnegie Institute of Technology. He decided to attend Carnegie Tech, for which his mother paid the first year's tuition with postal savings bonds Andy's father had accumulated. Paul was no longer living at home, and John was helping with the household bills by selling Good Humor ice cream.

College Trouble

Andy soon ran into trouble in his university classes. He still spoke with a strong Eastern European accent, and had difficulty making himself understood. Nor could he write grammatically: he relied on two classmates, Ellie Simon and Gretchen Schmertz, to help him write his papers.

But even in art classes, despite his obvious talent, Andy had problems. He kept coming up with things he hadn't actually been asked to do for an assignment, and his work wasn't what professors were used to seeing. Several times his freshman year he was on the verge of flunking out of the university for failing to maintain the necessary standards.

Andy found yet another woman to help him out, this one the department secretary, Lorene Twiggs. He played on her sympathy, telling her how difficult things were at home, and making sure to always dress in worn-out clothes. However, at home his mother was feeding him very well indeed and complaining because he wouldn't wear a hat to keep his head warm.

At the end of Andy's freshman year, the art department had to drop many freshman students to make room for veterans returning from the just-ended Second World War. Only fifteen of the forty-eight students in

Andy's class survived the cuts, and with his poor grades, he wasn't one of them.

Andy burst into tears. Mrs. Twiggs put up a fight for him with the faculty, and they decided to let him stay on probation. He was to produce new work over the summer and then reapply for admission in the fall.

That summer he improved his grades in his non-art classes. Meanwhile, he took a sketchbook with him while he helped out his brother Paul three or four mornings a week, selling fruits and vegetables door to door. The lightning-fast sketches he produced of the people they saw in the streets earned him readmission to the art department—and won him a forty-dollar prize, the first cash he'd ever earned with his art.

The summer art prize drew new attention to Andy, and he fell in with a group of friends, both male and female, who were, in Warhol biographer Victor Bockris's words, "striking, stimulating . . . a noisy, outspoken, argumentative, high-spirited bunch."[7] They helped protect and nurture the rather childlike Andy through his remaining college years.

Throughout those years, Andy discovered many different forms of art. He joined the student film club. He attended symphony concerts. He became interested in ballet, and even took a modern dance class.

He went to parties. "He glowed," remembered Leonard Kessler, part of his group of friends. "You could see the little cherubic face lighting up."[8] It was another foreshadowing of the life he would one day lead in the nightclubs of New York.

In his main course of study, Andy was being taught by his instructors in the Painting and Design faculty that fine art and commercial art were one and the same thing: that the distinction between them was entirely artificial. It was a philosophy heavily influenced by the Bauhaus and it, in turn, heavily influenced Warhol in the years to come.

In the summer of 1947, Warhol and five other students rented a studio, the carriage house of an old mansion. They each had their own space to work in. Andy did a series of paintings of children on swings and little boys picking their noses.

The Blotted Line

Sometime while he was at Carnegie Tech, Andy developed the drawing technique that would make his commercial art unique—and very successful—when he

The Bauhaus

"Das Stattliches Bauhaus" was created in Germany at the end of the First World War by Walter Gropious. It was an institute for experimenting with and educating a new generation of designers in architecture, industrial art, and handicrafts. At its heart was an ideology that said art and technology should be integrated, to the benefit of both.

The goal was to combine the previously separate roles of artist and craftsman, and apply the resulting aesthetic to everything from architecture to household appliances to typefaces.[9] The Bauhaus made art a business—and so, too, would Andy Warhol, many years later.

moved to New York a few years later. He would first copy a line drawing onto a piece of non-absorbent paper, then hinge that paper with tape to a second sheet of more absorbent paper. He'd ink over a small section of the drawn lines on the first sheet with an old fountain pen, then fold over the second piece of paper and lightly press it to the first to absorb or "blot" the ink. Large drawings had to be done in sections, which made it a very time-consuming process. The resulting image was unique, with dotted, broken and delicate lines. The blotted image could then be colored in various ways.[10]

Sometimes Andy would use images from magazines in these drawings, tracing a chair from a photograph, then using the blotted-line technique to transfer his tracing to a new piece of paper.

His art continued to be controversial. A painting showing a woman nursing a dog was removed from a department exhibition because one of the faculty objected. In March 1949, a painting he submitted to the annual Pittsburgh Associated Artists exhibition, showing a little boy with his finger up his nose, was rejected after half the jurors thought it was insulting. The other half thought it was an important work. The scandal drew even more attention to Andy's work.

Also during his years at Carnegie Tech, he began experimenting with changing his name. He was art director of the university literary magazine, *The Cano*; for that, he called himself Andrew Warhola. But on his self-designed Christmas card, he signed his name as André. He sometimes signed paintings Andrew Warhol, but to his friends he was Andy Warhol. Eventually, that was what he settled on.

In 1948, when he was nineteen years old, Warhol got his first commercial art job painting backdrops for windows in Joseph Horne's, a prominent Pittsburgh department store. He used some of the money to make his first trip to New York with fellow art students Philip Pearlstein and Art Elias to look at modern art, and see if there were any job opportunities.

Tina Fredericks, the art director of *Glamour* magazine, liked his portfolio and promised him work as soon as he graduated. She later recalled the first time she

Andy Warhol (far left) in 1949 with the Modern Dance Club at the Carnegie Institute of Technology.

saw him: "I greeted a pale, blotchy boy, diffident almost to the point of disappearance but somehow immediately and immensely appealing. He seemed all one color: pale chinos, pale wispy hair, pale eyes, a strange beige birthmark over the side of his face . . . His ink lines were electrifying. Fragmented, broken, and intriguing, they grabbed at you with their spontaneous intensity."[11]

At dinner, George Klauber, who had left Carnegie Tech the year before, told Warhol and Pearlstein that he was sure commercial artists could make it in New York and offered to share his contacts with them if they moved to the city.

After he graduated, though, Warhol wasn't entirely certain he wanted to go to New York. He worried about moving away from his mother. For a while he considered becoming a high school art teacher. According to his brother, John, he sent his portfolio to a school in Indiana, and only when they rejected him did he firmly decide to go to New York.[12] He was helped in that decision by Pearlstein, who said he would go with him.

New York, New York

Just one week after graduation, in June 1949, Warhol and Pearlstein moved into a shabby apartment in what was essentially a slum on New York's Lower East Side. It was a momentous moment in American art history, though of course no one knew it at the time. Both men would go on to be leading figures in very different art movements—Pearlstein in contemporary realism and Warhol in pop art.

At the time the leading movement in New York art circles was abstract expressionism, "a painting movement in which artists typically applied paint rapidly, and with force to their huge canvases in an effort to show feelings and emotions, painting gesturally, non-geometrically, sometimes applying paint with large brushes, sometimes dripping or even throwing it onto canvas."[13] Among the most famous abstract expressionists were Jackson Pollock and Willem de Kooning. The artists themselves sometimes got into fights over painting at the Cedar Bar, where they liked to hang out. It was close to where Warhol and Pearlstein lived, but they didn't really fit in there.

In any event, almost no one could make a living as a fine artist. The real money was in commercial art, as the economy rebounded in the postwar years and advertising became big business.

True to her word, Tina Fredericks gave Andy work, hiring him to draw shoes for *Glamour*. Those shoes launched his commercial career, and a highly successful one it proved to be. It also made him a New York fixture. His friends called him "Raggedy Andy" because of his slightly rumpled appearance but Warhol seemed to have gotten further by playing on his seeming sweetness and naiveté.

Art directors of the time were influenced by the Bauhaus, just as Andy's university instructors had been. They liked the way Andy's commercial art seemed to show that he was having fun, that he wasn't somehow lowering himself to draw pictures of shoes and clothes and furniture. "The impression he left was of this eager, interested person, who drew beautifully," recalled George Klauber.[14]

Work started to pour in. Andy drew for *Glamour*, *Charm*, and *Seventeen*. He did album covers for Columbia Records. He worked hard. But he still felt like an outsider, someone on the fringes of the beautiful celebrity world he'd long aspired to.

Near the end of the summer of 1949, not long after Andy turned twenty-one, *Glamour* published his first drawing, of girls climbing a ladder to illustrate an article on finding success in New York. The credit listed his name as Andy Warhol, and Andy Warhol he would be from then on.

At the end of their first summer in New York, Pearlstein and Warhol moved into a new apartment, just as full of cockroaches as their first one. At about the same time, more of Warhol's friends from university days arrived in New York. Some of them said he shouldn't waste his talent on commercial art and should be painting more. It didn't seem to faze Warhol, who didn't see a big distinction between the two.

In March 1950, Warhol and Pearlstein and the people they'd been subletting from were all evicted from their apartment. Pearlstein was about to get married to Dorothy Kantor, also a Carnegie Tech artist, and so he and Warhol parted company. Warhol moved into a two-bedroom basement apartment near Central Park, where he lived with a group of dancers. Despite the noise and confusion, he worked constantly, usually at night, sometimes not eating breakfast until the afternoon.

His roommates remember him as being sweet, charming, painfully shy, and interested in celebrities. "He would write fan letters to Truman Capote and Judy

Garland," said Elaine Baumann, one of the dancers who shared the space. "He would be breathless when he'd seen Somebody or Someone."[15]

In the fall of 1950, the dancers and Warhol had to move out when their building was slated for demolition. He moved in with another classmate from Carnegie Tech, Joseph Groell. Groell returned to Pittsburgh that winter for several months, leaving Warhol on his own for the first time.

Meanwhile, his work continued to draw attention. He'd done book jackets. He'd even appeared on television—or at least, his hand had. NBC would show it on the morning news program, drawing the weather map.

A piece he'd drawn of a sailor injecting heroin, published in a full-page ad in *The New York Times* on September 13, 1951, promoting a radio documentary, earned him more money than anything else he'd ever done, and was used on the cover of the recording of the program. In 1953, Warhol won the Art Director's Club gold medal, the top award in the advertising art industry.

His assignments grew more prestigious. He illustrated Amy Vanderbilt's *Complete Book of Etiquette*. He was able to buy better clothes, but he kept the same rumpled, edge-of-poverty look when he visited art directors.

A Secret Life

Warhol's personal life was complicated by the fact that he was a homosexual. In the 1950s, homosexuality was both against the law and unacceptable in mainstream society. Even though he found his way into the homosexual

underground, guided to the right parties and the right
bars by George Klauber, he was more interested in its
glamour than in sex. Through most of his life, Warhol
seems to have been interested in sex more as an observer
than as a participant. He once said the most interesting
thing about sex was not doing it. He tended to form
crushes on beautiful but unavailable young men, and
often complained about his "boy problems." [16] When he
did form close relationships with men, they inevitably fell
apart after a few months.

In 1952, Warhol finally moved into his own
apartment, a cold-water basement flat in a building
located right under the tracks of an elevated train. He
wasn't very good at taking care of himself: his clothes
were falling apart, he had holes in his shoes, and he was
mainly living on cake and candy. Shortly after that,
Warhol's mother Julia moved in with him. She would
continue to live with him until just before she died. With
her there to take care of the house, Warhol was able to
focus on his work. On June 16, 1952, Warhol's solo
show of illustrations based on the stories in Truman
Capote's book *Other Voices, Other Rooms*, published
while Andy was still in high school, opened at the Hugo
Gallery. It was his first tentative step out of the world of
commercial art into the world of fine art. Unfortunately,
it was also, essentially, a flop.

The director of the Hugo Gallery in 1952 was
Alexander Iolas who, ironically, would also be
responsible for Warhol's last exhibition, in January
1987. Normally the gallery wouldn't have put on a
show so late in the season, but Iolas was impressed

enough with Andy's work to make an exception. Unfortunately, because it was so late in the season almost every important person in New York's art community, including Iolas himself, was in Europe when *Fifteen Drawings Based on the Writings of Truman Capote* opened. The show ran from June 16 to July 3, 1952.

The pictures were delicate drawings of boys, butterflies, and cupids, with splashes of magenta and violet. "The work has an air of precocity, of carefully studied perversity," wrote James Fitzsimmons in a review in *Art Digest*.[17] But very few people saw it, although Truman Capote himself and his mother, Nina, showed up before the show closed, much to Warhol's delight.

None of the pieces, priced at around three hundred dollars, sold, but Andy had made a very important contact in David Mann, the gallery manager. Mann went on to work for the Bodley Gallery, mounting three Warhol shows between 1956 and 1959, "which I loved doing," Mann said, "but they were always kind of crazy."[18]

In the spring of 1953, Warhol's burgeoning commercial career took another leap forward when he obtained an agent, Fritzie Miller. With her help, Warhol landed assignments with magazines like *McCall's*, *Ladies' Home Journal*, *Vogue*, and *Harper's Bazaar*. "Whatever he illustrated—shampoo or bras or jewelry or lipstick or perfume—there was a decorative originality about his work that made it eye catching," *New Yorker* art critic Calvin Tomkins wrote in 1970.[19]

Warhol, just twenty-five years old, was becoming the most sought-after illustrator of women's accessories in

artist on John Cheever's "Vega" ANDY WARHOL

Hello mr lynes

thank you very
much

biographical information

my life couldn't fill a penny post card

i was born in pittsburgh in 1928 (like

everybody else in a steel mill)

i graduated from carnegie tech

now i'm in N Y city moving from one

roach infested apartment to another.

Andy Warhol

Warhol wrote this letter in 1949 to editor
Russell Lynes.

New York—and beginning to make a lot of money doing it. However, he had a tendency to waste money on extravagances like breakfast at the Plaza Hotel or expensive pastries. Finally able to afford a better place to live, he sublet a fourth-floor apartment from his former classmate Leonard Kessler, with the understanding that Kessler, a children's book illustrator, would be allowed to continue to use one of the smaller rooms for several months as a studio. Warhol moved in, along with his mother and many cats.

Warhol's friends enjoyed his old-country mother, with her folksy style and broken English. She looked after Andy, shopping for him, making him sandwiches, sorting and mending his clothes, urging him to go to church, and always getting after him, and his visitors, to "work, work, work."

While he certainly took her advice about working, his friends seldom saw him following his mother's advice to go to church. He did, however, wear a cross on a chain around his neck and carried his own pocket missal and rosary.[20]

The same year he moved to Lexington Avenue, Warhol began a brief affair with Alfred Carlton Willers (who preferred to be called Carl), a twenty-year-old from Iowa. They met in the photo collection of the New York Public Library, and Willers became a frequent visitor to Warhol's apartment, although Julia Warhol thought he was just a friend. Although Willers and Warhol remained friends for many years, their physical relationship was short-lived. Warhol later said that he was twenty-five when he had his first sexual experience, and twenty-six when he stopped. And Willers himself said, "[W]hen I knew him for all intents and purposes he was already celibate."[21]

It was Willers who suggested that Warhol, who was very sensitive about the fact he was going bald, begin wearing hairpieces.[22] For the rest of his life he was seldom if ever seen without a wig.

"Everything Was Wonderful"

Warhol continued to try to break into the world of fine art. In 1954 he had three shows at the Loft Gallery. He was part of a group show in April, then followed that up with a one-man show consisting of marbled paper sculptures with small figures drawn on them, then a show made up of drawings of a dancer, John Butler. Art directors from all the major advertising agencies attended the opening, but the show was almost ignored in the fine-art world.

At the Loft Gallery Warhol met Vito Giallo, assistant to the well-known graphic artist Jack Wolfgang, in whose studio the gallery operated. Shortly afterward, Warhol hired Giallo as his first assistant. Giallo enjoyed being around Warhol. "He was always positive about everything in life," he said. "Everything was wonderful."[23]

Everything became even more wonderful that autumn when Warhol fell in love with Charles Lisanby, a set designer for both television and Broadway. The two met at one of the innumerable parties Warhol attended. "He was interested in the fact that I was working in television and because other very fine artists like Ben Shahn worked in television occasionally," Lisanby said.

"Andy wanted to do that. Andy always wanted to do anything that was going to get him publicity. . . . The one thing then that he wanted more than anything else was to be famous."[24] The relationship cooled after a trip around the world together in 1956.

In 1955, Warhol got his biggest commercial account of the 1950s, doing a weekly ad in the Sunday *New York Times* for a Manhattan shoe store, I. Miller. The ads were a huge success for the store and made Andy famous within the advertising community. That fall Warhol replaced Vito Giallo with Nathan Gluck, who would be his assistant for the next nine years. He also had his first show at the Bodley Gallery, where David Mann had gone after leaving the Hugo Gallery. Reviewers were not impressed and only a couple of drawings sold, at very low prices. Nevertheless, Mann was able to get some of the drawings included in the *Recent Drawings* show at the Museum of Modern Art.

In 1956, Warhol's living arrangements changed again. He rented a second-floor apartment in the building where he and his mother were living, leaving his mother in the fourth-floor apartment they'd been sharing. With his own carefully (if sparsely) decorated space, Warhol began throwing his own parties. He also began collecting art. Occasionally his brothers would visit, bringing their children with them.

In December of that year, Warhol's fine art made something of a breakthrough with his *Crazy Golden Slippers* show at the Bodley Gallery. The show featured large blotted-line paintings of shoes painted gold, or decorated with gold metal and foil. Each was given the name of a celebrity: Judy Garland, James Dean, Julie Andrews, etc. The show was featured in a two-page color spread in *Life Magazine*. Great publicity, but *Life* described him as a "commercial artist" who had created the pieces "as a hobby."[25]

Today, the *Crazy Golden Slippers* show is seen as heralding the attempt to bridge "high" and "low" culture that was central to Warhol's work throughout his career. In 2008, one of the untitled pieces from the *Crazy Golden Slippers* show sold at auction for $205,000. In its notes for the piece, the Doyle New York auction house says that Warhol "took the concept of 'kitsch' [an inferior and trashy knock-off of something of greater artistic value]" and "endowed it with a language-like structure that brings it into the realm of high art . . . the *Golden Slippers* series transcends utilitarian function to embody the artist's fantasy life of celebrity."[26]

By 1957, Warhol was so successful financially that he established Andy Warhol Enterprises on the advice of his accountant. He had another very successful show at the Bodley Gallery, called *Gold Pictures*. But he was still seen as just a commercial artist, not a serious one.

An Earthquake in Art

In the "serious" art world, the rules were changing, as two new artists, Jasper Johns and Robert Rauschenberg, led a move away from abstract expressionism. Like Warhol, Rauschenberg, who was also a commercial artist, embraced popular culture and rejected the angst and seriousness of abstract expressionism. Looking for a new way of painting, he started using unusual materials and methods, painting with house paint, for example, or putting ink on a car tire and then running it over paper. He had his first solo exhibition at the Leo Castelli Gallery in 1959, exhibiting works that had moved away from abstract paintings to what he called combines: three-dimensional collages. His combine *Monogram*, for instance, combined a stuffed angora goat, a tire, a police barrier, the heel of a shoe, a tennis ball, and paint.[27]

Jasper Johns, who worked with Rauschenberg in New York on window displays for Tiffany's, created paintings of targets, maps, and flags. Leo Castelli discovered Johns's work while visiting Rauschenberg's studio, and was so impressed he offered him a show on the spot—a year before Rauschenberg's own show.[28]

That first Johns show, titled *Flags, Targets and Numbers*, sold out. The Museum of Modern Art bought four pieces. Instead of the intense personal vision of the abstract expressionists, Johns took commonplace objects and painted them in such a way that, as he put it, "There may or may not be an idea, and the meaning may just be that the painting exists."[29]

Like Warhol, Rauschenberg and Johns began as commercial artists. They'd worked for some of the same people Warhol had: they'd all designed windows for Tiffany, for instance. Unlike Warhol, they'd been immediately taken seriously. But if they could do it, Warhol figured, so could he.

Warhol began going regularly to the Leo Castelli Gallery, where Johns and Rauschenberg had been shown, hoping to break in. Johns and Rauschenberg were also homosexual, but they wanted to distance themselves from the gay community. They never associated with Warhol, who later said that one of their mutual friends told him that Johns and Rauschenberg disapproved of him because his art was too commercial and his behavior "too swish." That is, he was too openly and flamboyantly homosexual, in an era when, far more than today, homosexuals were looked down on or openly reviled by straight society.[30]

At about the same time Johns and Rauschenberg made their big splash, Warhol met Emile de Antonio, an artist's agent who was also interested in film and who would become famous later as a documentary director.

Tina Fredericks of *Glamour*, who introduced de Antonio to Warhol, described him as "a catalyst who could, almost miraculously, put his finger on what direction talent ought to take." According to Fredericks, Warhol credited de Antonio with being the first person he met who saw "commercial art as real art and real art as commercial art, and he made the whole New York art world see it that way, too."[31]

But Warhol's last show of the 1950s, *Wild Raspberries*— watercolors of fanciful foods, with make-believe recipes hand-lettered under each image by Warhol's mother— didn't have much impact. He still wasn't being taken seriously, and nobody wanted to publish an accompanying book of recipes and drawings. Warhol self-published it and tried to sell copies himself, but nobody wanted them.

As the end of the 1950s wound down, then, things weren't going very well for Andy Warhol. He'd bought a townhouse and moved into it with his mother. But then

Gallery owner Leo Castelli stands in his gallery in the 1960s. Surrounding him are pieces of art from other famous artists including Jasper Johns and Robert Rauschenberg.

he lost his profitable I. Miller account, which suddenly left money in much shorter supply, requiring him to do more commercial work right when he wanted to concentrate on his art.

Warhol later claimed he had a nervous breakdown in 1959. He consulted a psychiatrist for a short time. His depression seemed centered on one thing: his desire— and apparent inability—to break through into the world of fine art and the accompanying fame.

Pop Art Arrives

The new art that Johns and Rauschenberg were leading the way toward had a name: pop art. It had begun in London in the mid-1950s, then made its way to New York. One textbook describes it this way: "The Pop artist turns outward to his environment—not the natural environment, but the artificial one of mass popular culture—finding his material in the manipulated and programmed folkways and the mass-produced commodities of modern urban and suburban life." Pop art, in a reversal from the traditional view, "accepts and approves the art (such as illustration and comic strips) and artifacts of mall culture as entirely valid art in themselves."[32]

Warhol loved pop art, and hated abstract expressionism, but he had to find his own subjects and technique. He did a series of black and white paintings of sections of cheap advertisements for wigs and cans of food. Then he did a series of large paintings of comic strip characters such as Dick Tracy and Popeye. In the summer of 1960, he tried something new: a realistic, black-and-white painting of a Coke bottle, about six feet tall. He also painted a Coke bottle with elements of abstract expressionism in it. He showed both to de Antonio, who told him he should destroy the abstract expressionist version and show the other one. "It's our society, it's who we are, it's absolutely beautiful," de Antonio said.[33]

In addition to transforming his art at about this time, Warhol transformed himself. He bought some new silver-blond wigs, and wore them uncombed and slightly off-center. He took to mumbling short, not-always coherent replies to questions. He exaggerated his limp wrists and the mincing way he walked—the "swish" mannerisms Johns and Rauschenberg objected to. According to his biographer Bockris, his image—the one most people associate with Warhol to this day—was based on a combination of Marlon Brando and Marilyn Monroe. It was a defensive strategy: no one could make fun of him because he had already made fun of himself.

Ivan Karp, the assistant to Leo Castelli (whose gallery Warhol so much wanted to be shown in), came to look at the new paintings and told Warhol the only ones he thought mattered were the cold, straightforward ones like the Coke bottle. He took some slides back to the gallery because he thought some people who were interested in another new painter, Roy Lichtenstein, also might be interested in Warhol. Karp brought a few collectors to Warhol's studio, and he sold a few paintings—though for far less than he could make for any commercial assignment.

Lichtenstein was also working with comic book images—but his paintings were far more powerful than Warhol's. Karp had no luck trying to get gallery owners to show Warhol's work. A lot of people didn't like his work. For others, it was personal.

Among those uninterested was Leo Castelli. He didn't think he could show Warhol when he was already interested in Lichtenstein: the two were working in a similar fashion, but Lichtenstein was better. "You're mistaken," Warhol told him in his office. "What I'm doing will be very different from what anybody else is doing. . . .You will take me. I'll be back."[34]

Without a gallery to represent him, Warhol showed his paintings where he could, putting a handful on display for a week in a Bonwit Teller's window display, behind mannequins wearing the latest spring dresses and hats.

Then, late in 1961, Warhol confided in Ted Carey (one of his assistants) and interior designer Muriel Latow that he was desperate. "Muriel, you've got fabulous ideas," he told Latow. "Can't you give me an idea?"[35]

Latow said that she could, but it would cost him fifty dollars. He gave her the money. She suggested what he liked most in the world: money. "You should paint pictures of money," she said.

Warhol thought that was a great idea. And then she told him he should paint "something you see every day and something that everybody would recognize. Something like a can of Campbell's Soup."

"Oh!" said Warhol. "That sounds fabulous!"[36]

So that's exactly what he did.

Chapter 3

Pop Goes the Factory

While his soup cans were being shown in Los Angeles, Warhol was turning out canvas after canvas at home in New York, painting more Coke bottles, coffee cans, S & H Green Stamps, and more Campbell's Soup cans. He began experimenting with repetition, the same image appearing over and over in one picture. He also began to move away from brushes and paint to a new technique: silkscreening.

Drawing on his own collection of celebrity pictures, Warhol did silkscreen paintings of Elvis Presley, Troy Donahue, Warren Beatty, and Natalie Wood. Then, upon hearing the news that Marilyn Monroe had committed suicide on August 4, 1962, the same day his Campbell's Soup can show closed in Los Angeles, he did a series of portraits using a Marilyn Monroe publicity photograph taken by Gene Korman for the 1953 movie *Niagara*. He painted the background, eye shadow, lips, and face, and then applied the silkscreened image. In all, he did twenty-three of the paintings. The colors were garish

49

Warhol's Silkscreening

The silkscreening method Warhol used began with a photograph or drawing taken by himself or someone else. The photo was sent to a commercial silkscreen shop, where the image was projected onto silk (or a silk-like fabric) stretched over a frame. The fabric was coated with a light-sensitive emulsion that hardened when it was exposed to light. In areas where the emulsion hadn't been exposed to light, the emulsion could be washed off, leaving clear fabric.

Once the silkscreen came back to Warhol's studio, he or an assistant would lay the screen on a canvas, apply paint or printer's ink to the screen, then push a rubber blade called a squeegee across the screen, forcing the paint through those areas not blocked by the hardened emulsion.

Sometimes the canvas was hand-painted in advance with solid color backgrounds or spots of color to define lipstick or eye-shadow on a portrait. Although Warhol occasionally painted on top of the silkscreened image, usually the colors came first, then the silkscreen.[1]

and often didn't line up properly with the photographic image. In artspeak, they were "off register."

The most famous of the paintings is known as the Marilyn diptych: one hundred repetitions of her face across twelve feet of canvas.

The Monroe pictures seem to have been some sort of catalyst for Warhol's creativity. He silkscreened all the paintings he had done earlier that summer—dollar bills, coffee cans, Coke bottles, and soup cans. He turned a lurid tabloid headline ("129 DIE IN JET!") and accompanying photograph into a painting, projecting the

A museum visitor looks at Warhol's *Lemon Marilyn* that was painted in 1962.

image onto a canvas, then painting over it. In three months, he painted more than a hundred pictures. In total, in 1962, he painted two thousand that year. He was on fire—and he was about to set the art world on fire, too, because he finally had a New York gallery in which to show his work.

A New York Gallery at Last

The Stable Gallery was owned by Elinor Ward. She'd been forced to cancel a planned exhibition by artist Alex Katz scheduled for November 1962. Instead, she decided to show Warhol.

"Andy showed me this collection of work, and I was absolutely stupefied," she remembered. "It was an incredible collection."[2]

Just before the Stable Gallery exhibition, Warhol had three paintings in a group show that opened at the Sidney Janis Gallery on Halloween in 1962. Suddenly pop art was the talk of the art world. Then, a week later, Warhol's show opened.

Running from November 6 to 24, the show featured eighteen works, including some of the Marilyn Monroes, his *Do It Yourself* paintings, which looked like half-completed paint-by-number pictures, *129 Die*, and his serial images of Campbell's Soup cans.

This time, the critics took notice, with Michael Fried writing in *Art International* magazine that Warhol at his best, in the Marilyn Monroe paintings, "has . . . a feeling for what is truly human and pathetic in one of the exemplary myths of our time that I for one find moving."[3] However, he doubted the work would have lasting importance, an opinion that proved to be wrong.

In both subject matter and technique, there was nothing else like the show. It sold out even as people joked about how terrible it was. William Seitz bought a Marilyn for the Museum of Modern Art for two hundred fifty dollars. When one of his colleagues called him and said of the show, "Isn't it the most ghastly thing you've ever seen in your life?" Seitz answered, "Yes, isn't it. I bought one."[4]

The Public Face of Pop

Warhol spent most of the party after the Stable Gallery opening standing in a corner with a blank look on his face, barely mumbling when people spoke to him. Because of his odd appearance and behavior, and his art, Warhol became the primary target for everyone who wanted to attack pop art. But if there's no such thing as bad publicity, then that was certainly true of Warhol.

Every attack on him, including those by critics who hated the show, only enhanced his fame. It wasn't just abstract expressionists threatened by the new wave or certain critics who hated his art, though: so did many of his friends and his family. But Warhol professed not to care. He said his philosophy was, "Don't think about making art, just get it done. Let everyone else decide whether it's good or bad, whether they love it or hate it. While they're deciding, make even more art."[5] It was a philosophy he followed his whole career.

He also began to cultivate a very social lifestyle, going out to openings, dinner, or parties every night. By all accounts, the parties really took off when he arrived. For him, parties weren't just about fun: they were also work, the work of maintaining the image of Andy Warhol-the-pop-celebrity.

By June 1963, Warhol was making so many paintings he could no longer continue to work at home, so he rented a studio on the second floor of an abandoned firehouse a few blocks from his house. There was no heat, the roof leaked, there were holes in the floor, but it was cheap: about $150 a year. During that spring and summer, Warhol painted several more of his most famous portraits, including a series of six-foot-tall silver images of Elvis Presley holding a gun. He also hired a new assistant, Gerard Malanga, to help him with his silkscreens. Nathan Gluck continued to assist him on his commercial art work, which he relied on to pay the bills.

Warhol also worked on a series of paintings that had more in common with *129 Die* than the cheerful Coke bottles and soup cans. These were all based on images of violence: car crashes, suicides, an electric chair. He silkscreened newspaper photographs onto canvases covered with garish colors, and gave the paintings names like *Vertical Orange Car Crash* or *Lavender Disaster*. He put his creativity into the concept and design: once he had decided what the piece should look like, it took only four minutes to complete. Mistakes were inevitable working at that speed, but Warhol saw the mistakes as part of the art. It was at this time that he famously told *Time* magazine, "Paintings are too hard. Machines have less problems. . . . I'd like to be a machine, wouldn't you?"[6]

Of course, people saw Warhol's paintings as some kind of social commentary, although he always denied it, saying he simply found the images interesting. They weren't the wisest choice financially speaking. Today they sell for millions apiece, but at the time very few people wanted them. Who wants to hang a painting of a car crash on the wall? As a result, Warhol had no one-man shows in New York in 1963, despite the success of his 1962 show. However, these would eventually prove to be the paintings that made him famous in Europe.

Even without a one-man show, Warhol's career continued to develop in 1963. He began making films. And in November he moved his painting equipment from his home to the fifth floor of a warehouse and factory building.

Birth of the Factory

Warhol's new studio space was a single room, about one hundred feet long and forty feet wide. Four metal pillars

The Jackie Kennedy Portraits

On November 22, 1963, President John F. Kennedy was assassinated by Lee Harvey Oswald in Dallas, Texas.

Warhol retreated into his "I'd like to be a machine" pose in his public response: "It was just something that happened. It isn't for me to judge."[7]

However, his artistic response was quite different: he took eight newspaper photographs of Jackie Kennedy, the president's widow, taken just before and after the assassination, and morphed them into a large, sixteen-panel work in blue and grey.

The work was never shown in New York full scale, but it has been shown in Europe, where, said art critic Frank O'Hara, it was "absolutely moving and beautiful."[8]

supported the low ceiling. It had a concrete floor and crumbling brick walls. It had previously been a hat factory, and it was about to become a factory again. But not just "a" factory: "the" Factory, one of the most famous locations in the New York art world.

The first things produced there were another of Warhol's most famous works: four hundred sculptures of grocery boxes for Campbell's tomato juice, Kellogg's cornflakes, Del Monte peach halves, Brillo pads, and other products, made out of plywood and silkscreened to look as much like the originals as possible.

Elinor Ward at the Stable Gallery, who had refused to show Warhol's paintings of violence, wasn't too excited about the idea of a show made up of boxes. But Warhol eventually convinced her, saying they would sell for three hundred to six hundred dollars each.

Warhol and Malanga got to work on them. It took three months. Warhol described his typical schedule during this time

> We usually worked till around midnight, and then we'd go down to the Village, to places like the Cafe Figaro, the Hip Bagel, the Kettle of Fish, the Gaslight, the Cafe Bizarre, or the Cino. I'd get home around four in the morning, make a few phone calls . . . and then when it started to get light I'd take a Seconal, sleep for a couple of hours and be back at the Factory by early afternoon.[9]

While the work was under way, a twenty-one-year-old hairdresser and lighting designer named Billy Linich (later known as Billy Name) started renovating the studio. The color scheme was simple: silver.

While Linich worked on the Factory, a lot of his friends started coming by regularly. They were mostly flamboyantly gay, with nicknames like Rotten Rita, the Sugar Plum Fairy, Mr. Clean, the Duchess. They were also mostly amphetamine ("speed") users, and were sometimes called the "amphetamine rapture group" or "the mole people," the latter because, like most gay people, they remained underground during the 1960s. Their nickname for Warhol was "Drella," a mixture of Dracula and Cinderella.

Warhol himself had started to take amphetamines, prescribed by his doctor, which was one reason he needed to take Seconal, a barbiturate, each night—it counteracted the speed and let him sleep. However, he was never a heavy drug user, unlike many of the people who surrounded him throughout his life.

The Factory in 1965. The walls were covered in aluminum foil to keep the "silver" theme that Warhol wanted.

Warhol also changed the way he looked, favoring a black leather jacket, tight black jeans, T-shirts, high-heeled boots, dark glasses, and a silver wig to match the décor.

In April 1964, just before his *Boxes* show opened at the Stable Gallery, Warhol had a disagreement with Philip Johnson, the architect who had commissioned murals from various artists, including Warhol, to decorate the outside of the American pavilion at the New York World's Fair being held in Flushing Meadows that summer. Warhol created a twenty-foot-square black and white piece entitled *The Thirteen Most Wanted Men*, which made use of the mug shots of criminals. Art critic and Warhol biographer David Bourdon suggests "the state of being 'wanted'—it didn't much matter why one was wanted—obviously had an appeal for Andy."[10] But on April 16, after objections to Warhol's work from the governor of New York (who thought it might be insulting to Italians because most of the wanted men were Italian), Johnson told Warhol he had just twenty-four hours to replace or remove it.

Warhol silkscreened twenty-five identical images of Robert Moses, the city's planner and president of the Fair, to replace the "most wanted men," but Johnson rejected that idea. Finally, Warhol simply ordered the panels to be painted silver.

"In one way I was glad the mural was gone: now I wouldn't have to feel responsible if one of the criminals ever got turned in to the FBI because someone had recognized him from my pictures," Warhol wrote later. The silkscreens of the wanted criminals didn't go to waste, though: he went ahead and did paintings of them, noting that they "certainly weren't going to get caught from the kind of exposure they'd get at the Factory."[11]

Boxes

Just five days after Philip Johnson's ultimatum, on April 21, 1964, Warhol's *Boxes* show opened at the Stable Gallery. It looked like the interior of a warehouse with boxes of canned goods stacked all over, making a kind of maze that was difficult to get through. The press picked up on the fact that the designer of the original Brillo box, which quickly became the most recognizable image from the show, was himself a painter, the abstract expressionist James Harvey. Warhol called Harvey and offered to trade one of the sculptures for a signed original box, but Harvey died of cancer before the trade could be arranged.

The same day the *Boxes* show opened at the Stable Gallery, Warhol held a party at the Factory. White, red, and green spotlights lit up the silver that covered everything—aluminum foil on the walls and ceiling and pipes, silver paint on the floor and everything else, right down to the toilet bowl. Rock music blasted.

According to Victor Bockris, the party marked a turning point in Warhol's career. It was the last time he was photographed in a group with other famous pop artists like Lichtenstein. Warhol was moving away from being famous as an artist, and toward being simply famous.

But being famous wasn't making Warhol rich. Few of the boxes sold. "We all had visions of people walking down Madison Avenue with these Campbell's Soup boxes under their arms, but we never saw them," remembered gallery owner Elinor Ward.[12]

Shortly after that, Warhol moved to the Castelli Gallery, where he'd wanted to be shown since the Jasper Johns show.

Meanwhile, the Factory had become *the* place to be. As David Bourdon described it,

> The place functioned as a combination clubhouse, community center, lounge, and cruising area for some of New York's more outlandish type—preening fashion models, ranting amphetamine heads, sulky poets, underground moviemakers, and imperious magazine editors, as well as wide-eyed college students and occasional movie personalities and rock stars. . . . Soon, professional photographers

from all over the Western world were also hanging
around the Factory, the new frontier of artistic
far-outness.[13]

Poets held poetry readings at the Factory. Actors put
on plays. There were always parties. Warhol shot his
films there. But somehow, he also managed to create art.
His first show at Castelli, in November 1964, featured
paintings of flowers, based on a color photo of hibiscus
blossoms taken by Patricia Caulfield, which he had seen
in a magazine. Caulfield eventually sued Warhol for
using her photograph without permission. After a long,
costly court case, Warhol agreed to give her several
paintings, and a percentage of all profits from future
reproductions, in payment. After that, for fear of being
sued again, Warhol mostly took his own photographs.

In a marked contrast to his previous couple of shows,
the flower paintings sold out. *Newsweek* profiled Warhol.
The critics were generally positive. As always, though,
they were ambivalent toward Warhol himself, whose
primary focus increasingly seemed to be his own fame.
He used to spend every morning on the phone talking to
his press agent, telling him everything he had done.

Controversies simply added to Warhol's image.
Warhol had several one-man exhibitions outside the
United States in 1965, including Paris, France; Milan
and Turin, Italy; Essen, West Germany; Stockholm,
Sweden; Buenos Aires, Argentina; and Toronto, Canada.
The Toronto show, scheduled to open on March 18,
attracted controversy when Charles F. Comfort, the
director of the National Gallery of Canada, refused to
certify that the boxes were works of art. As a result,

they were subject to a duty of 20 percent—sixty dollars on each of the three-hundred-dollar boxes, eighty of which were being brought in for the show. Warhol expressed indifference, as he usually did. "It really doesn't matter much to me—I don't care much," he told *The Globe and Mail* newspaper.[14]

Warhol Retires

In May 1965, Warhol made his first trip to Europe since he had become famous, for the opening of his flower paintings at the Sonnabend Gallery in Paris. The show broke attendance records. French critics praised Warhol. And then Warhol dropped a bombshell: he told the French press that he was retiring from painting to make films.

Of course, Warhol had every intention to paint more: just not right away. According to Victor Bockris, the announcement was a carefully planned strategy to increase the prices of his paintings: the flower paintings were selling for as little as two thousand dollars. Warhol figured if he stayed away from painting for a while, the prices would increase. Besides, Bockris said, "Andy felt the pop-art explosion was spent."[15]

As a result, Warhol's next show at the Castelli Gallery, which ran from April 2 to 27, 1966, was conceived as his "farewell to art."

Castelli's assistant, Ivan Karp, had suggested to Warhol that he paint something "pastoral, like cows," so he wallpapered one room of the gallery with repeated images of a cow's head. He filled the second room with free-floating helium-filled silver pillows.

Pop artists in the mid-1960s, from left to right: Tom Wesselman, Roy Lichenstein, James Rosenquist, Andy Warhol, and Claes Oldenberg.

According to Ronnie Cutrone, a young art student and dancer who hung out at the Factory and would eventually become Warhol's assistant, "Andy said he wanted to end his painting career with those silver pillows, to let them fly away from the rooftop, but they didn't really fly away. It was a grand gesture; he was a master of the grand gesture."[16]

There were few sales. Warhol would not have another major show at Castelli's until 1977. Warhol's attention had turned elsewhere, into the worlds of film and music. And what he produced there proved to be just as groundbreaking and controversial as his art.

Chapter 4

Warhol the Filmmaker

Warhol's childhood interest in movies carried over into his adult life, so it wasn't too surprising that as his art career developed he began to think about expanding into that medium. He was helped in that decision by his friendship with Emile de Antonio. He went to lots of mainstream Hollywood films, but he also viewed a lot of experimental films at the Film-Makers' Cooperative.

"They're so terrible," he told poet John Giorno. "There are so many beautiful things. . . . Why doesn't somebody make a beautiful movie?"[1]

In July 1963, Warhol bought a Bolex 8-mm movie camera for twelve hundred dollars. The first "beautiful movie" he decided to make was one of Giorno sleeping. Warhol shot about four hours of footage a night over two weeks, only to discover he had ruined it all because he had failed to rewind the camera properly. It wasn't an auspicious beginning to a filmmaking career, but Warhol persevered, filming the whole movie again. Several more months would pass while it was edited.

Much of *Sleep* was made by looping (repeating) some of the same footage over and over, a technique which connects it to Warhol's use of repetition in his static art. Black and white and silent, it was shot at the standard speed of a sound film (twenty-four frames per second) but projected at the silent speed of sixteen frames per second, which meant that not only was it a six-hour film of someone sleeping, it was a six-hour film of someone sleeping *in slow motion*.

"Sleep begins with a 20-minute scene of Giorno's belly," wrote Lavanya Ramanathan of the *Washington Post*. "Followed by Giorno on his back. Then there is some quality time with Giorno's armpit. Then something else—perhaps a knee?" Unlike in real life, Ramanathan noted, "no one ever complains they just didn't get enough *Sleep*."[2]

Giorno, with whom Warhol was sexually involved at the time, recalled that the news Warhol had made a movie triggered all kinds of publicity. "It was absurd," he said. "He was on the cover of *Film Culture* and *Harper's Bazaar* before the movie was finished!"[3]

The film premiered on January 17, 1964, at the Grammercy Arts Theater. It was a benefit screening for the Film-Makers' Cooperative, but it couldn't have been much of one: only nine people attended, and two of them left during the first hour.

Warhol's second film was a short documentary called *Andy Warhol Films Jack Smith Filming Normal Love*. Smith was a controversial underground filmmaker who would later appear as an actor in several other Warhol films, as would many of his actors. "I picked something

The Los Angeles Premiere of *Sleep*

Warhol longed to be a Hollywood producer, so he must have been pleased to hear that when *Sleep* made its debut in Los Angeles at the Cinema Theatre about five hundred people turned out. Unfortunately, things went downhill from there.

The film began running at 6:45 P.M. The first people walked out at 7 P.M. Not long after that, they began walking out and asking for their money back, despite the "No refunds" sign. The theater manager, Mike Getz, finally agreed to give out free passes for another show, and handed out more than two hundred. By the time the film dragged to its close, only fifty people were left.

Getz noted that, ironically, one problem with the screening of *Sleep* was that some of the sleeping was being done by the projectionists. However, to be fair, he also noted that of the few people who stuck it out, some were "really digging the movie."[4]

up from him for my own movies—the way he used anyone who happened to be around that day, and also how he just kept shooting until the actors got bored," Warhol said.[5]

One of his actors was Taylor Mead, who in late September 1963 accompanied Warhol and others on a cross-country car trip to the opening of the Elvis exhibit at the Ferus Gallery. While he was in Los Angeles, Warhol filmed scenes for another film, *Tarzan and Jane Regained . . . Sort of*, featuring Mead and an actress named Naomi Levine, who was the first person to appear naked in an Andy Warhol film. She wouldn't be the last.

Constant Filming

For the next few years, Warhol was always filming
something. Eventually, there would be more than two
hundred films with his name on them. His next "major"
film after *Sleep* was *Kiss*, which featured a series of
couples, many of whom were not at all compatible in
real life, posing in a mouth-to-mouth kiss, held for three
minutes without moving. The films were originally
shown as individual segments, one a week. *Haircut* was
like *Sleep*, only it featured a haircut. It was also much
shorter. So was *Eat*, which featured a man eating a
mushroom.

Warhol said he made these films the way he did,
with a stationery camera focused on a single actor doing
the same thing over a long period of time, because he
thought people usually went to the movies to see only
the star, to "eat him up." "Here at last is a chance to
look only at the star for as long as you like," he said.
"It was also easier to make."[6]

Jonas Mekas, a pioneer avant-garde filmmaker, a
founder of Anthology Film Archives and an early supporter
and presenter of Warhol's films, put it this way:

> You watch a Warhol film without being hurried. . .
> . The camera hardly moves from the spot. It remains
> focused on the subject as if there were nothing
> more beautiful and important than this subject. We
> can look at it longer than we are accustomed to. . . .
> We begin to understand that we have never really
> seen what happens when hair is cut or how one
> eats. . . . The whole reality of our environment
> suddenly becomes interesting in a new way.[7]

Warhol decided to try his hand in filmmaking in the mid-1960s. Here, he lines up a shot using a 16mm Bolex camera.

Empire and *Screen Tests*

It wasn't long before Warhol decided to take the same approach to filming but with a much more monumental subject: the Empire State Building.

Filmed from 8:06 P.M. on July 25 to 2:42 A.M. on July 26, *Empire* is a single static shot of the famous skyscraper. The film begins with a totally white screen. As the sun sets, the image of the building emerges. Floodlights come on. Interior lights flicker on and off for the next six and a half hours. Then the floodlights go off, and the remainder of the film takes place in, essentially, total darkness.

Empire was shot with a new piece of equipment, an Auricon newsreel camera that had sound capability. Originally there was to be talking in the background, but Warhol changed his mind and decided to keep it silent. At the premiere of *Empire*, people walked out, booed, and threw paper cups at the screen. In Malanga's words, *"Empire* was a movie where nothing happened except how the audience reacted."[8]

Writing in 2008, Mary Woronov, who appeared in Warhol's later films, said it took her forty years to

> realize that Andy never meant to do a film. He was doing a painting. Pop art put the image back in painting and Andy took it even further and put the image on film instead of canvas. . . . [T]hese films were never meant to screen in a theater, where I thought they were boring. They were meant to hang on a wall. They are Andy's greatest paintings.[9]

From early 1964 through November 1966, Warhol shot some five hundred *Screen Tests*. Visitors to the Factory were seated in front of a camera on a tripod and asked to be as still as possible and not blink while the camera was running.

The subjects ran from various Factory denizens through celebrities such as poet Allen Ginsberg and musicians Bob Dylan, Lou Reed, and David Bowie. Some of the footage was compiled into longer films with titles like *The 13 Most Beautiful Boys*, *The 13 Most Beautiful Women*, *50 Fantastics*, and *50 Personalities*. In 1966 Warhol and his assistant, Gerard Malanga, put together a book featuring *Screen Test* stills of seventeen women and thirty-seven men, along with Malanga's poetry. *Screen Tests/A Diary* was published by Kulchur Press in 1967.

Warhol's Superstars

Warhol tended to use the same people over and over in his films. They became what he called "superstars," although in general he paid them nothing for their work. They cooperated just to be part of the Factory scene, and because Warhol kept promising them that someday they'd be big, that they really *would* be superstars.

Warhol's first "superstar" to attract a lot of media attention was Jane Holzer, nicknamed Baby Jane. The daughter of a wealthy real estate magnate, Holzer went into modeling and became famous when she appeared in the English version of *Vogue* magazine in the summer of 1963. She was married to the extremely wealthy Leonard Holzer. When Jane Holzer was introduced to Warhol, he asked if she'd like to be in a movie he was making called *Soap Opera*. Shortly afterward she invited Warhol to dinner at her father-in-law's house. Also attending were Mick Jagger and Keith Richards of the Rolling Stones, which became Warhol's favorite rock band.

Soap Opera, the first film Holzer did for Warhol, was the first Warhol film to be mentioned in the *New York Times*. Holzer eventually appeared in several Warhol movies, and also allowed Warhol to escort her to parties, gallery openings, and rock shows, which attracted a lot of press attention, much to Warhol's delight. She tended to avoid the Factory, though; she didn't like the drug use among the people who hung out there.

Poor Little Rich Girl

Unlike Jane Holzer, other Warhol superstars didn't have the slightest problem with drug use at the Factory. In fact, it was just what they were looking for. During the filming of more than two hundred films, Warhol used a lot of people. The most famous of his superstars was Edie Sedgwick.

Soap Opera had been subtitled "The Lester Persky Story" because it included television commercials produced by Persky, the man who introduced hour-long commercials, what today are called "infomercials," to television in the 1950s. It was Persky who introduced Sedgwick to Warhol in January 1965.

Sedgwick, who had grown up on a ranch in California, came from a family with a history of mental problems and had already suffered some of her own. She began hanging out regularly at the Factory in March 1965 with Chuck Wein, whom she had met in Cambridge, Massachusetts, and who was determined to make her a star. During one of those visits, Warhol used her in his movie *Vinyl*. After that, she starred in *Poor Little Rich Girl*, which consisted of her lying on her bed, talking on the phone and showing off her clothes, explaining how she had spent her entire inheritance in just six months. Warhol started taking Sedgwick everywhere. They were photographed as a couple with Lady Bird Johnson, the wife of President Lyndon Johnson, at the opening of a show called *Three Centuries of American Painting* at the Metropolitan Museum of Art. When Warhol went to Paris for the opening of his

Warhol poses in front of a movie screen showing Edie Sedgwick, who starred in many of Warhol's films.

show at the Sonnabend Gallery that April, he took Sedgwick and Wein with him. When he got back, he asked his scriptwriter, Ron Tavel, to write a script for Sedgwick to star in. "Something in a kitchen. White and clean and plastic," was his direction. The resulting film was called, not too surprisingly, *Kitchen*. In it, three people sit around a table in a small kitchen talking about nothing in particular. Most of the dialogue can't be heard, anyway. At the end, Sedgwick's character is killed for no apparent reason.

The film got a lot of attention, with Norman Mailer proclaiming that "it captured the essence of every boring, dead day one's ever had in a city. . . . . I suspect that a hundred years from now people will look at *Kitchen* and say, 'Yes, that is the way it was in the late Fifties, early Sixties in America.'"[10]

Kitchen was the last film Ron Tavel wrote for Warhol, though he contributed a few scenarios from time to time. Sedgwick's promoter, Chuck Wein, pushed Tavel out, and was credited as writer and assistant director on the next film starring Sedgwick, *Beauty No. 2*. It featured her sitting in her underwear on her bed with a man, called Gino, in jockey shorts, drinking vodka while being questioned off camera by Chuck Wein. Through the course of the film Sedgwick gradually falls apart emotionally.

When *Beauty No. 2* premiered on July 17, some critics compared Edie Sedgwick to Marilyn Monroe in her onscreen presence. That excited Warhol; he thought she could be his ticket to the big time of moviemaking. Sedgwick was with Warhol on October 8, 1966, for the

Ron Tavel: Warhol's "Screenwriter"

Once Warhol had a camera that could record sound, he realized he was going to need something he'd never needed before in a movie: dialogue.

Warhol had seen a writer named Ronnie Tavel at a Wednesday-night poetry reading at the Cafe Le Metro. He invited Tavel to the Factory to sit in a chair off-camera and talk while he shot his first movie with sound, *Harlot*, starring Mario Montez.

Tavel continued to write "scenarios" for several months. His films with Warhol included *The Life of Juanita Castro*, *Horse*, *Vinyl*, *Hedy*, and *Kitchen*. He even wrote a musical, called *Piano*, but that project fell through.

Each film was different, but a description of how *Horse* was filmed indicates just how different a "script" for a Warhol film was from a screenplay for a standard Hollywood movie:

> Tavel's task in the case of *Horse* was to get 66 minutes of film footage from four unprepared and intimidated young men . . . and a horse. To accomplish it, Tavel devised a scheme in which he wrote the names of the actors on four placards and all the action and lines of dialogue on what he called cheat sheets. These latter were ordered in some semblance of a plot and would be held up in sequence by Warhol's assistant Gerard Malanga on cue from Tavel, who moved about the periphery of the set and held up the placard bearing the name of one of the four actors, chosen in accordance with how he saw the story evolving. Seeing his name on Tavel's cue card, the designated actor would turn to Malanga and read his line.[11]

opening of a retrospective of Warhol's art at the Institute of Contemporary Art in Philadelphia.

The curator, Sam Green, painted the floors silver and put on loud rock music in an attempt to make the gallery look like the Factory. He succeeded a little too well. More than two thousand people, many of them students, jammed a space intended to hold no more than seven hundred. Fortunately, Green must have had some inkling of what could happen, since he took all the paintings down before the opening for fear they would be damaged.

Some students were injured when they were pushed through plate glass windows. The campus security guards had to escort Warhol, Sedgwick, and the rest of his entourage to a balcony overlooking the gallery for a brief appearance, then cut a hole in the ceiling so the Warhol group could escape onto the roof and down a fire escape to the street, where the police had to rescue them.

Warhol and Sedgwick had become icons of the 1960s, but Sedgwick was becoming increasingly erratic and was fighting with the Factory gang. Her last film with Warhol was *The Death of Lupe Velez*, filmed in December 1965.

One reason Sedgwick's time was winding down at the Factory was that she believed people outside Warhol's circle who told her she didn't need him anymore. Chief among those was Bobby Neuwirth, often called the "right-hand man" of singer Bob Dylan, whom Sedgwick had met even before she met Warhol.

Sedgwick had been led to believe she had a chance to star in a film with Dylan or be promoted as a singer.

When she found out during an argument with Warhol at a restaurant in February 1966 that Dylan had secretly married Sarah Lownds in November of the previous year, she went to make a phone call. When she came back she announced that she was leaving the Factory.

Sedgwick was featured in one of the photographs on the inner sleeve of Bob Dylan's album *Blonde on Blonde* released on May 16, 1966. Some people thought some of Dylan's songs were about her, including the famous "Like a Rolling Stone."

The Dylan film never materialized for Sedgwick; neither did a singing career. She tried modeling after leaving the Factory, and auditioned for a Norman Mailer play. After a stint in a mental hospital, she moved back to Manhattan. She'd been taking drugs for years, and she continued to do so.

Sedgwick's final film wasn't a Warhol film. Called *Ciao! Manhattan*, it tells the story of young "Susan Superstar" as she parties her way through Manhattan as a Warhol superstar. The film is set in the character's parents' mansion in Southern California, and the story is told through a series of flashbacks comprised of film footage from a previous, unfinished project. Combining scripted segments with audio interviews carried out while Sedgwick was high on drugs, it ends with the headlines announcing Sedgwick's death in 1971.

Many people blamed Warhol for Sedgwick's death. She'd implied more than once that he was the one who had gotten her hooked on drugs. In fact, of course, she was on drugs and had plenty of other problems before she ever met Warhol, but being in his circle certainly didn't help matters.

Even before her death, Sedgwick's friends weren't happy with Warhol. One of them, the poet Gregory Corso, came up to Warhol's table in a club called Max's one night in 1967 and told him, "I know you, mister, and I don't like you. I know all about how you use people. How you make them superstars of New York and then drop them. You're evil. . . . You give them dope and then you leave them."[12] Warhol pretended not to hear.

"Andy was destructive because he didn't give, he gave nothing, and that's what Edie had been complaining about," wrote playwright Robert Heide, who said that when shown the spot where Freddie Herko, another of Warhol's "superstars," had committed suicide by dancing out of a window, Warhol commented, "When do you think Edie will commit suicide[?] . . . I hope she lets us know so we can film it."[13]

The Velvet Underground

Warhol's films changed when Paul Morrissey, a former social worker who hated to be around drugs and had been very much a film traditionalist, emerged as Warhol's right-hand man. He wanted to make commercial films and managed to convince Warhol that his own films could be profitable.

Morrissey also looked for ways to market Warhol's name. In mid-December 1965, he convinced theater producer Michael Myerberg to call his new discotheque Andy Warhol's Up, and said Warhol could also provide the music. That meant, of course, that Warhol needed to find a band, and as it happened, one had recently presented itself: the Velvet Underground, led by singer/guitarist/songwriter Lou Reed. Warhol heard them play at Club Bizarre, and afterward met with Reed and invited the band to the Factory.

Shortly after that, the singer/actress Nico returned to New York and got in touch with Warhol's assistant, Gerard Malanga. Warhol proposed adding her to the Velvet Underground. She would be his next superstar.

First, of course, he had to convince the Velvet Underground that they needed Nico. She really just wanted a backup band, and they had no interest in being just a backup band. But Warhol was offering to manage them, give them a place to rehearse, finance their equipment, support them, and make them famous—in return for 25 percent of their earnings.

In the end, the band agreed to Morrissey's suggestion that Nico sing some songs, but not all. It helped that Nico liked Lou Reed and Reed liked Warhol.

"It was like bang!" remembered actress Mary Woronov. "They were with Andy and Andy was with them and they backed him absolutely. They would have walked to the end of the earth for him. And that happened in one day!"[14] They even agreed to change the name of the band to the Velvet Underground and Nico.

The Velvet Underground performed as part of a week of mixed-media shows Warhol presented in February at the Film-Makers' Cinematheque. Called *Andy Warhol*

Uptight, and intended as a kind of dress rehearsal for the new disco, it featured the band and Nico performing while the Warhol films *Vinyl*, *Empire*, and *Eat* were screened in the background. A new film, *More Milk, Yvette*, was premiered. While the band played, a group of interpretive dancers pretended to shoot up heroin, whip each other, and perform crucifixions.

That same month Warhol appeared on television and officially announced he was sponsoring the Velvet Underground.

Andy Warhol Uptight never played at the club Andy Warhol Up; the manager there had changed his mind. Instead, it morphed into the *Exploding Plastic Inevitable*, which first played a dance hall called the Dom. Warhol himself ran the film and slide projectors and changed the light filters, essentially conducting everything that happened.

Critics' reactions to the show, probably the first multi-media show ever staged in New York, were good, and it came just when Warhol's "farewell to art" show, featuring the cow wallpaper and floating silver balloons, opened at Castelli's.

It looked like Warhol had made the right decision to "retire" from painting. His film *My Hustler* had just opened and had become the first Warhol film to make a profit. The *Exploding Plastic Inevitable* brought in eighteen thousand dollars in its first week. Warhol had started working on a Velvet Underground and Nico album.

Morrissey handed over management of the *Exploding Plastic Inevitable* to booking agent Charlie Rothchild, who took the whole show on the road to Los Angeles, where it promptly fell apart, done in by internal disagreements and a fierce rivalry between the East and West Coast music scenes. Warhol returned to New York. However, the *Exploding Plastic Inevitable* would continue to tour, minus Warhol, for several more months.

Chelsea Girls

Warhol's finances, which had looked so promising just recently, were now in bad shape: the Velvet Underground experiment had lost him money rather than making any. Though it was hard for people to believe, looking at his lifestyle, he was actually making less money in the 1960s than he had as a commercial artist in the 1950s.

Warhol had discovered, after being commissioned to do a portrait entitled *Edith Scull 36 Times*, that painting portraits was a fairly easy and reliable way to make money. That summer he did a few more to finance the rest of his activities. For the rest of his career, his portraits—photographs silkscreened on pre-painted canvasses—would be a major source of his income.

Beginning in mid-June 1966, Warhol had his best three months of filmmaking. He shot fifteen one- and two-reel films during that time. They had no plots. They mostly had no scripts. They were shot in one take, until the thirty-five-minute reels ran out. Warhol liked the idea of simply pointing the camera at people and waiting for something to happen. This put a lot of pressure on the performers, most of whom were using drugs.

Since films need tension, Warhol and Morrissey would prime the actors ahead of time with nasty rumors, playing them off against one another in order to get interesting "performances." The results were raw, sometimes violent, but very real. It also led to many of the performers despising each other in real life.

When they reviewed the footage, Warhol and Morrissey realized the films could be made to relate to each other. They assembled twelve of them into a six-and-a-half-hour film called *Chelsea Girls*.

That was too long, so Warhol decided to show two reels side by side on a split screen with sound coming from only one side at a time. Some of the films were color. Some were black and white. The overall effect, at least for some people, was mesmerizing.

Chelsea Girls proved to be Warhol's first commercial success, costing just fifteen hundred to three thousand dollars to make and grossing one hundred thirty thousand dollars in its first nineteen weeks in New York, where it opened on September 15. Several of its participants became famous: Ondine, Nico, International Velvet (Susan Bottomly), Brigid Berlin, and Mary Woronov. They even got paid, sort of: they were each eventually given one thousand dollars to sign a release.

Reviews in the national press led to the film being booked in other cities. Warhol got great publicity when the theater showing the film in Boston was raided by the vice squad and the manager fined two thousand dollars on four charges of obscenity.

A Hard Life at the Factory

Just before *Chelsea Girls* opened, one of the performers in the *Exploding Plastic Inevitable*, Danny Williams, committed suicide. When Williams's mother called the Factory, Warhol refused to speak to her.

Drugs were taking their toll on many members of Warhol's Factory set. So was the constant atmosphere of infighting and jockeying for position. But Warhol pressed on making movies. He even made one starring his mother, Julia, in her basement apartment, as an aging movie star with a lot of husbands.

As 1967 began, Warhol was working on three new films similar to *Chelsea Girls*, with the same actors and improvised dialogue. One of them, *Vibrations*, was planned to be forty-eight hours long, although it would run for "only" twenty-four hours on a split-screen like *Chelsea Girls*. Despite the problems at the Factory, more actors arrived there to work on Warhol's films, including a young man named Allen Midgette, who would later pretend to be Warhol at various events.

In March, MGM released the *Velvet Underground and Nico* album. Production was delayed partly because of the Warhol-designed cover, which featured a banana that could be peeled. The album didn't do well at the time, although it still sells steadily today. Newspapers and magazines wouldn't carry any ads for it, since some of the songs dealt with controversial subjects like drug use. Most radio stations wouldn't play it. In fact, the reaction was so negative Lou Reed didn't play again in New York until 1970. He also began looking for a new manager. Worse from Warhol's point of view was the fact he made no money from the album.

Movie shooting wasn't going smoothly, either, but at least Warhol looked forward to a May trip to the Cannes

Andy Warhol

Warhol designed the album cover for the Velvet Underground in 1967.

Film Festival to show *Chelsea Girls*. The three-week trip was supposed to be his payment to some of his superstars for appearing in his films, but it proved to be a disaster: *Chelsea Girls* was not shown after all. When Warhol got back to the States, he flew to a Velvet Underground concert in Boston with Paul Morrissey and Nico, only to find Lou Reed had hired a new manager. Nico wasn't permitted to sing with the band. It was the end of Warhol's connection to the Velvet Underground.

In July 1967, the Hudson Theater started running Warhol's *My Hustler*. Warhol's fame as a filmmaker was starting to grow, and the film drew well. The manager called up Paul Morrissey and asked him if they had anything else. He asked for a film like Warhol's *I, a Woman*. Warhol decided instead to shoot *I, a Man*. It was a feature-length comedy, and was followed by two other comedies, *Bike Boy* and *Nude Restaurant*.

But the thing that really sets *I, a Man* apart is that it features a performance by a woman named Valerie Solanas. According to Warhol actress Ultra Violet, during the course of shooting *I, a Man*, Solanas, a lesbian, said to her, "Love can only exist between two secure, freewheeling, groovy females. Love is for chicks. Why do you let him exploit you? Why don't you sink a shiv into his chest?"[15]

With that attitude, it's not surprising Solanas headed up, and was the only member, of an organization called SCUM, the Society for Cutting Up Men, which called for the elimination of men in the interest of world peace. In 1968, Solanas came very close to eliminating Andy Warhol.

Chapter 5

The Shooting of Andy Warhol

Warhol liked Solanas's performance in *I, a Man*: he found her honest and funny. But Solanas complained about Warhol. Talking to him, she said, was "like talking to a chair."[1]

Nico also appeared in *I, a Man*. Warhol had pushed her to record a solo album, but he was getting tired of her. She was on drugs and spending a lot of time with other celebrities, including Jim Morrison, Bob Dylan, and Brian Jones. She wasn't as focused on Warhol, or on her Warhol-driven career, as he wanted her to be. Warhol's next superstar was Viva (Susan Hoffman), who appeared in *Bike Boy* and *Nude Restaurant*, the two comedies that followed *I, a Man*.

Other things were changing, too. Paul Morrissey had gone so far as to install cubicles in the Factory, making it more businesslike. Warhol's longtime assistant, Gerard Malanga, was getting restless. He would eventually leave the Factory that summer.

Billy Name, who had created the Factory's silver look and managed the place like a theater, saw that Morrissey was taking over. He was also wondering when he would get anything more than the ten dollars a week (and a place to live) he'd been paid since he started.

In fact, the whole feel of the 1960s started changing in 1967. That summer—the so-called "Summer of Love"—there were riots in Detroit, a recession, and a surge in organized crime centered on the lucrative drug trade. "The sixties had lost their edge and their bloom," is how Ondine put it. "It was beginning to get very decadent very, very quickly, and it became very grim."[2]

Annoying Students Nationwide

That fall, Warhol started a tour of college campuses, with a program deliberately designed to annoy his audiences. The students turned out to hear Warhol speak, and Warhol refused to say a word. Typically he'd show a segment of the incredibly boring *The 24 Hour Movie* (also known as ****), then, as Viva described it,

> stood on the stage, blushing and silent, while Paul Morrissey, the professor, delivered a totally intellectual anti-intellectual rapid-paced fifteen minute mini-lecture putting down art films, hippies and marijuana, saying things like 'At least heroin doesn't change your personality.' Then I . . . answered questions—'The reason we make these movies is because it's fun, especially the dirty parts'—and advised them to drop out of school. Then I would rant about everybody in authority.[3]

85

Students often responded by hissing and booing. Warhol got into even more trouble later in the year when he sent Allen Midgette to colleges in Utah and Oregon to impersonate him at public appearances. It took four months for anyone to notice. After that, he had to go the colleges for real to make up for the deception.

Warhol had no use for hippie culture. He thought the hippies were ripe to be taken over and told what to do. He was beginning to get attacked from those on that side of the counterculture who thought he was just a hustler, out to make money, and had "sold out."

By this time, many people did not like Warhol. Some of it came from his own people. His film *Imitation of Christ* was released in November—and withdrawn after one showing. The same thing happened with *The 24 Hour Movie*, which premiered in mid-December. Warhol's superstars were furious that films they'd worked on for a year, which Warhol had promised would make them famous, ended up simply being discarded.

Warhol and his superstars were getting attacked in the press, too. *Time* art critic Robert Hughes wrote, "They were all cultural space-debris, drifting fragments from a variety of sixties subcultures. . . . [I]f Warhol's superstars . . . had possessed talent, discipline, or stamina, they would not have needed him. But then, he would not have needed them. They gave him his ghostly aura of power."[4]

Even though things weren't going that well on many fronts for Warhol in 1967, one positive event was the arrival of Frederick W. Hughes at the factory. Although he was just the son of a traveling salesman from

Houston, Hughes portrayed himself as an aristocratic snob. Before long, Hughes was running the business end of things for Warhol. The one thing Hughes did for Warhol right away was sell a lot of his earlier, mostly ignored paintings, like the death-and-disaster scenes. Then he started landing portrait commissions for Warhol, each one priced at twenty-five thousand dollars. And that meant that, for the first time, Warhol's painting could actually pay his bills.

Hints of Violence

Violence hovered around the edges of the Factory. Occasionally, it made a center-stage appearance, as on the night in November when a friend of Ondine's, called Sammy the Italian, ran in with a gun, lined Warhol and others up on the couch, and told them he was going to play Russian roulette. He put the gun to Paul Morrissey's head and pulled the trigger. Nothing happened. Nico got up to leave, and he pointed at the ceiling and pulled the trigger again. This time it fired.

At one point Sammy put a woman's plastic rain hat on Warhol's head, made him kneel on the floor, and said he was going to take a hostage. Actor Taylor Mead jumped Sammy from behind, and after a struggle Sammy ran away.

When the police arrived, they didn't take the attack seriously. Neither did the newspapers. *The New York Times* wasn't at all sure the attack had happened, and even if it had, said "it wouldn't be an important story anyway." "The real thud was that no one cared about us," said Billy Name.[5]

At the beginning of 1968, Warhol took his entourage to Arizona to film a movie called *Lonesome Cowboys*. They didn't exactly fit in with the conservative Southwest, and a simulated gang rape in the film led to an official complaint to the FBI, which placed Warhol under surveillance. The FBI suspected he was about to commit the crime of interstate transportation of obscene material. They eventually concluded no crime had been committed.

Viva was the star of the movie, and was beginning to believe she really was the superstar Warhol treated her as. She was also in love with Warhol. At one point she proposed that they get married. He refused. Then, in mid-February 1968, she became so furious she threw her handbag at him, hitting him in the side of the face. *Nobody* hit Warhol. That was the end of her time as a superstar.

A New Factory

One of Warhol's first tasks after returning to New York from Arizona was moving the Factory. Its building on 47th street was being torn down. The new location was the sixth floor of the eleven-story Union Building. During the move, the big curved couch that had been the central piece of furniture in the old Factory, and therefore featured in many films, was stolen.

The change was more than just a change in location. "For one thing, the Silver Period was definitely over, we were into white now," Warhol wrote. "Also, the new Factory was definitely not a place where the old insanity could go on. . . . [T]he big desks up front as you came in off the elevator gave people the hint that there was something going on in the way of business, that it wasn't all just hanging around anymore."[6]

Gerard Malanga, who was off in Rome showing his own movie—and almost getting arrested for trying to sell fake Warhols—was replaced by a new manager, Jed Johnson. In part, the new more business-like Factory was a reaction to the Russian roulette incident at the old one. Warhol perhaps had an inkling of the danger inherent in his old way of doing things, but he couldn't escape his old circle of acquaintances that easily. In particular, Warhol couldn't escape Valerie Solanas. Robert Marmorstein of the *Village Voice* interviewed Solanas that winter. She called Warhol a "son of a [expletive]" and said every word that came out of his mouth was a lie—but she also claimed he was still planning to produce a script she had given him before he had gone to Cannes.[7] Warhol got handed a lot of material like that, and he usually accepted it in the spirit of encouraging the writer, but he never had any intention of producing it.

When he came back from Cannes, Solanas wanted her script back. Warhol told her he had lost it. After that, she started calling regularly, demanding money. When she also started making threats, Warhol quit taking her calls.

Meanwhile, very little new work of any sort was being produced. *Lonesome Cowboys* was still undeveloped and unedited. Warhol let Paul Morrissey go ahead with a project he wanted to do, called the *Surfing Movie* or *San Diego Surf*. Warhol took his cast and crew out to La Jolla, California, and rented a mansion for a three-week shoot. The police kept a very close watch on them. Once again there was a great deal of friction on the set, particularly between Viva and Paul Morrissey. Warhol himself was detached. The film was never released.

As Warhol flew back to New York, Valerie Solanas was in the process of buying two guns.

The Shooting of Andy Warhol

On Monday, June 3, 1968, Warhol spent the morning talking to Fred Hughes on the phone. Hughes had a frightening story of violence to tell Warhol: he'd been mugged the night before.

At 2:30 P.M., Valerie Solanas went to the Factory. She'd become convinced Warhol was conspiring against her with Maurice Giordias, publisher of Olympia Press, who had given her an advance of six hundred dollars to write a novel based on her SCUM manifesto.

Told Warhol was out, Solanas waited outside. When Warhol finally arrived at the Factory at 4:15 P.M., she joined him and Jed Johnson, who was carrying some fluorescent lights. They entered the building together. Warhol noticed that Solanas was wearing a thick turtleneck sweater under a trench coat, even though it was a hot summer day. She was also wearing makeup, something which, as a radical feminist, she *never* wore. She seemed on edge, and kept twisting a brown paper bag in her hands.

Up in the Factory, Fred Hughes was writing a memo at his desk and Paul Morrissey was talking on the phone to Viva, who was at the hairdresser's having her hair done in preparation for a role in the film *Midnight Cowboy*. Meanwhile, Mario Amaya, an art critic and curator, was waiting for Warhol so he could discuss an upcoming retrospective in London.

When the elevator arrived, Morrissey handed the phone to Warhol (Viva was still on the line). Johnson went into Warhol's private office. Warhol had just signaled Hughes to pick up the phone and carry on the conversation with Viva when Solanas pulled a .32 automatic from the paper bag. She fired a shot at Warhol, which missed.

Viva, hearing the gun firing over the phone, thought someone had cracked a whip.

Warhol screamed, "No! No! Valerie! Don't do it!"[8] but she fired a second time. She missed again. Warhol flung himself on the floor and tried to crawl under a desk, but her third shot connected.

The bullet entered through his right side, tearing through his lung, then ricocheting through his pulmonary artery, esophagus, gall bladder, liver, spleen, pancreas, and intestines before exiting his left side, leaving a large hole. He felt "a horrible, horrible pain, like a cherry bomb exploding inside me."[9]

Thinking she'd killed him, Solanas fired her fourth shot at Amaya, who was crouching on the floor. She missed. She fired again, this time hitting him slightly above the hip; the bullet went through him without damaging any organs, though it missed his spine by only a quarter of an inch. He ran into the back room and threw his body against the doors to hold them shut.

FINAL

DAILY ⊞ NEWS
NEW YORK'S PICTURE NEWSPAPER ®

8¢

10¢ O TSIDE L.I. AND SUBURBS

Vol. 49, No. 296   Copr. 1968 News Syndicate Co. Inc.   New York, N.Y. 10017, Tuesday, June 4, 1968*   WEATHER: Sunny and warm.

ACTRESS SHOOTS
ANDY WARHOL
Cries 'He Controlled My Life'

Headlines from the *Daily News* shout that
Andy Warhol was shot.

Solanas then pointed the gun at Hughes. He begged her not to shoot him. She walked over to the elevator and pressed the button, then returned and aimed the gun at his forehead. She pulled the trigger, but the gun jammed. She pulled a second gun, a .22 caliber, from the brown paper bag, but then the elevator arrived. Instead of shooting Hughes, she left.

Hughes called an ambulance, and the police. Viva called back from the hairdresser's, wondering what was going on. Hughes told her Warhol had been shot and there was blood everywhere. Then he hung up. Thinking it was a joke, Viva went on with her hair appointment.

Just a couple of minutes after the shooting, Gerard Malanga showed up; he was supposed to pick up money to pay for a film announcement.

It took half an hour for the ambulance to arrive. It delivered Warhol to the emergency room of Columbus Hospital at 4:45 P.M. The doctors had no idea who he was. They did know he was in bad shape. At 4:51 P.M., Warhol was pronounced dead, but Amaya, who was on the table across the room, sat up and screamed, "Don't you know who this is? It's Andy Warhol. He's famous. And he's rich. He can afford to pay for an operation . . . do something!"[10]

Warhol was "dead" for ninety seconds while the doctors cut open his chest and massaged his heart. With it restarted, they began to operate, removing his ruptured spleen and working to repair as much damage as they could. The operation took five and a half hours.

While Warhol was on the operating table, at about 8 P.M., Solanas surrendered to a rookie traffic cop named

William Shemalix, handing over the guns and telling him she had shot Warhol "because he had too much control of my life."[11] With her arrest, Fred Hughes and Jed Johnson, who had been held for questioning, were released.

The Aftermath

The shooting shocked Warhol's family. Malanga took the subway to Warhol's townhouse after the shooting. Julia let him in. He was just in time to intercept a phone call from someone who had heard the news on the radio. After he hung up, he told Julia that Andy had been hurt, and he was going to take her to the hospital. Once there, when she found out just how badly he'd been hurt, she wept, "My little Andy, they hurt my little Andy." Because of her heart condition, hospital attendants put her in a wheelchair and took her to a private room.[12]

While Julia Warhola prayed for her "little Andy," his brother Paul was told by the doctor that there was only a fifty-fifty chance Warhol would pull through. Later his other brother, John, would say he didn't even realize how famous Andy was until Andy was shot and he saw all the headlines.

But the frontpage headlines were short-lived; even Warhol's knack for publicity had failed him. The night after Warhol was shot in New York, Robert Kennedy was assassinated in Los Angeles after winning the California primary. Warhol was then relegated to the inside pages.

On June 13, Warhol's doctors reported he was on his way to a complete recovery. Meanwhile, Solanas was sent for psychiatric evaluation. On June 28, she was indicted on charges of attempted murder, assault, and illegal possession of a gun. Her bail was set at ten thousand dollars.

Warhol would remain in the hospital throughout June and July. While he was there Ultra Violet asked him, "How do you explain it all? Why were you the one to get shot?"

"I was in the wrong place at the right time," he answered.[13]

Many of the follow-up press accounts were unsympathetic variations on the theme that "he had it coming." *Time*'s story, "Felled by Scum," was downright brutal. It began,

Andy Warhol in 1969.

> Americans who deplore crime and disorder might consider the case of Andy Warhol, who for years has celebrated every form of licentiousness. . . . [T]he pop-art king was the blond guru of a nightmare world, photographing depravity and calling it truth. He surrounded himself with freakily named people . . . playing games of lust, perversion, drug addiction and brutality before his crotchety cameras. Last week one of his grotesque bit players made the game quite real.[14]

Just about a year after the shooting, in June 1969, Solanas was sentenced to three years in prison. Since she'd already served one, she'd be out in two more years.

But John Warhola said the police told his brother that Solanas would go to jail for a long time if he appeared in court to testify against her. He chose not to because he was still recuperating. "He was real thin and weak," Warhola said. "He just thought he would never get better."[15]

Warhol was sent home on July 28, 1968. He spent his fortieth birthday on August 6 in bed. Warhol's brother John helped bathe his wounds and re-bandage them. By August Warhol, though weak, was back at work, painting a commissioned multiple portrait of Margaretta "Happy" Rockefeller, wife of the governor of New York. He appeared in public again for the first time on September 4.

"Since I was shot everything is such a dream to me. I don't know whether or not I'm really alive—whether I died," he said. And, he added, "I'm afraid. I don't understand why. I am afraid of God alone, and I wasn't before."[16]

Chapter 6

A Quieter Decade

Back at the Factory, Warhol conducted himself differently. He tended to stay in a tiny office off the main room, as far away as he could get from visitors arriving on the elevator. He did host a party in September for about two hundred guests, to celebrate the release of a new Nico album, *The Marble Index*, but in general he tried to avoid visitors unless he knew they were safe.

Strangely enough, security wasn't increased at the Factory as a result of the attack: anyone could still walk in through the door, which was guarded only by a receptionist and a stuffed dog. Things finally changed after 1972 when the Factory was robbed at gunpoint by two men. After that it was much harder to gain entry.

Some things at the Factory had continued without Warhol. Paul Morrissey was more in charge of the filmmaking than ever before. He'd shot the movie *Flesh* while Warhol was in the hospital. It cost four thousand dollars and ran for six months at the Garrick theater, and gained its star, Joe Dallesandro, a cult following. It also got better reviews than many Warhol films—possibly because Morrissey directed it, although Morrissey played down his involvement.

In October, Warhol himself was able to shoot another movie, eventually known as *Blue Movie*. It got its title not only because it contained explicit sex, but also because Warhol accidentally shot it indoors on outdoor film, which gave it a bluish tinge. It was the last movie Viva appeared in.

Warhol was worried about money again. His hospital bill of eleven thousand dollars had wiped out most of the profits of 1968. But one bright side of getting shot was that the price of his paintings had increased. Works that had originally sold for two hundred dollars were now selling for fifteen thousand. Hughes was able to sell more of Warhol's early work at the new prices, but Warhol was still focused more on filmmaking than painting.

Meanwhile, tape recordings Warhol had done with Ondine in 1965 and 1967 were being transcribed for a book to capitalize on the notoriety of his having been shot. Called *a: a novel*, the book was published by Grove Press in November, to generally bad reviews.

Shortly after the book was finished, Billy Name sequestered himself in his darkroom at the back of the Factory. He essentially lived there alone, practicing meditation, for a year, with the only evidence of his presence in the Factory the empty yogurt cartons and take-out food containers that appeared in the trash each morning.

In December, Warhol almost fainted when he answered the phone and heard Valerie Solanas on the other end. She wished him a Merry Christmas, and then said she'd shoot him again if he didn't meet her demands: she wanted to be on Johnny Carson's *Tonight Show*, she wanted her SCUM manifesto published in the *Daily News*, and she wanted twenty-five thousand dollars in cash. As a result of that call and threats to other people, she was locked away again and her bail increased, eventually to one hundred thousand dollars. She would remain in jail until the sentencing in June.

What Next?

Warhol seemed a bit lost in 1969, as though trying to figure out what to do next. *Lonesome Cowboys*, released in May, won the San Francisco Film Festival Award. Warhol continued to long to do a big movie, but Hollywood wasn't interested.

Warhol was also in pain from his wounds. One still needed to be drained regularly. He went back into the hospital in March for a follow-up operation to remove part of the bullet that had been left inside him. The doctors sewed his stomach muscles back together incorrectly, which forced him to wear a surgical corset for the rest of his life to keep his stomach from expanding too much when he ate. After that, Warhol refused to have anything to do with hospitals: he thought if he ever went into one again, he wouldn't come out alive.

Desperate for money, Warhol even rented a theater that summer and showed a series of pornographic films.

On a good day the theater brought in fifteen hundred dollars, but it made little profit, and Warhol soon gave it up.

Blue Movie opened on July 21. Warhol hoped it would be a huge success, but instead it was seized for being obscene. And far from generating respect, it got reviews like Rex Reed's: "Warhol is merely a joke now," he wrote. "He has contributed nothing of any real significance to the contemporary cinema."[1]

That fall, Warhol started an underground movie magazine called *Interview*. It didn't make much of an impact at the time, but it would become a major part of his business in the 1970s. In November, Billy Name finally left his darkroom, and the Factory.

Trash and Other New Ventures

The year ended with Warhol and Morrissey making their most expensive (twenty thousand to thirty thousand dollars) and most successful movie: *Trash*, starring Joe Dallesandro and, as his wife, the female impersonator Holly Woodlawn. Instead of being about sex, it was about drugs.

The actors earned twenty-five dollars a day. *Trash* eventually grossed $1.5 million. Warhol hoped to repeat the success with *Women in Revolt*, his next film, but when it finally opened in 1972, even though it got good reviews, it didn't make nearly as much money.

In 1970, an international traveling retrospective of Warhol's work was planned, but Warhol did not seem very interested. "I like empty walls," he said. "As soon as you put something on them they look terrible."[2]

Warhol shot *Trash* in 1969. The film starred Holly Woodlawn (left) and Joe Dallesandro.

In fact, he had every intention of returning to painting when the price was right. With one of his soup can paintings selling for sixty thousand dollars in May 1970, at that time the most ever paid at auction for the work of a living American artist, it appeared the price was beginning to be right.

Warhol started finding other ways to make money, too. He appeared with Sonny Liston in an advertisement for Braniff Airlines. He started investing in antiques, which became a lifelong passion: by the end of the 1970s he was obsessed with them, spending a million dollars a year on antique furniture and objects.

The renewed interest in Warhol the painter continued in 1971, but now it was international. The Warhol retrospective had opened in Paris in late 1970. In early 1971, it opened in London. In West Germany, collectors and museums sought Warhol's paintings and *Flesh* was one of the country's top ten films that year.

Warhol made a triumphant return to the New York art scene in April, when the Whitney Museum's version of the retrospective opened. The reviews were universally positive. That same month, his first play, *Pork*, opened off-Broadway. It went on to be a hit in London, where rock star David Bowie saw it. Bowie visited Warhol at the Factory, and Warhol inspired Bowie's Ziggy Stardust stage show. Bowie even hired many of the London cast members of *Pork* for it.

Warhol stepped further into the music world when he designed the cover for the Rolling Stones' classic album, *Sticky Fingers*, which featured the front of a pair of jeans with a working zipper. And he moved further into the realm of international—as opposed to national— celebrity status as a good friend of Bianca Jagger, wife of Rolling Stones lead singer Mick Jagger. He went antiques shopping with John Lennon, formerly of the Beatles, and his wife Yoko Ono. But although he had resumed going to parties every night, Warhol continued to be in pain from the shooting.

The Death of Julia Warhola

Julia Warhola's health went downhill after Warhol was shot. For a couple of years, they were both semi-invalids in the same house, with Jed Johnson looking after them.

Julia was slipping into senility, failing to take her medication and sometimes wandering away and getting lost. In February 1971, she had a stroke and was hospitalized.

When Julia got out of the hospital, Paul Warhola and his wife Ann took her to Pittsburgh, but it was difficult for them. She would get up every morning and claim she was going back to New York. By the end of a month, she didn't know where she was.

Then she suffered a second stroke and lay in the hospital in a coma for several weeks. She recovered enough to leave the hospital, but Paul and Ann were unable to care for her anymore, so they put her in the Wightman Manor nursing home.

Warhol called her every day from wherever he was, in America or Europe, but he never visited. When Julia talked about him, she spoke of him as a little boy. Throughout his life, she had continued to call him her little Andek.

Warhol was still shooting movies, and in 1972 he returned to painting with a series of more than two thousand paintings of Mao Tse-tung, the Chinese Communist leader. In addition to the familiar silkscreened-photo-over-color technique, he added hand-painted squiggles. Part of their effectiveness came from taking a potent symbol of Communism and turning it into just another mass-produced, capitalistic money-making item.

Simultaneously, Warhol produced a painting and print series called *Vote McGovern*, for George McGovern, the Democratic candidate in the 1972 presidential election, which actually consisted of a series of portraits of incumbent Richard Nixon in ugly color combinations. In September the newest Warhol film, *Heat*, was shown at the Venice Film Festival. Before its October opening at the New York Film Festival, one of its stars, Andrea Feldman, committed suicide.

As usual when someone near Warhol died, the press pinned part of the blame on him. Feldman left letters saying he had neglected her. In an interview before she died she said of working with Warhol and Morrissey: "They just throw you in front of a camera—they don't care what you look like. And they just use you, and abuse you, and step on you, and they don't pay you anything."[3]

The film cost between fifty thousand and one hundred thousand dollars to make, and took in $2 million in the United States. Critics generally praised it, but the star's suicide turned some of them off. Peter Schjeldahl wrote in the *New York Times* that "Miss Feldman, with her twisted little face and frightening laugh, was clearly in a bad way, and the pitiless exposure of her suicidal mood makes *Heat* a repellent document."[4]

In November 1972, Warhol's mother died in Pittsburgh. Warhol paid the funeral expenses, but he didn't attend the funeral. "Andy didn't want to see nobody dead," said his brother Paul. "He was deathly afraid."[5]

"I think he always felt guilty that he hadn't taken care of her until the end, but he couldn't have," said Jed Johnson.[6]

Warhol didn't mention his mother's death to his friends. Johnson didn't find out about it until 1975, when he asked Paul's son James how his grandmother was doing. As late as 1976, when asked about his mother, Warhol would reply, "Oh, she's great. But she doesn't get out of bed much."[7]

Warhol painted his mother's portrait a couple of years later. It appeared on the cover of *Art in America* in January 1975. His brothers both wanted copies, but he refused.

"No one ever fully comprehended her reasons for following Andy to New York," wrote David Bourdon in his biography of Warhol. "Had she needed Andy as much as he needed her? Clearly, she had been a major source of her son's tenacity, shrewdness, resilience, and playful humor, and she had obviously enjoyed her reputation as 'Andy Warhol's Mother.'"[8]

In one of her last interviews before she left New York, Julia Warhola said,

> I'm so glad I'm his mother. He's great. That I did that, you know, that's really a creation, don't you think it's a creation to produce Andy Warhol? I, Mrs. Warhol, I sometimes don't believe it that I could do that. But you see all the things he does, the good and the bad and the lousy and the shocking . . . and the fairies and the girls and the boys and the drugs. It's all here, it's all in him and he pours it out and he gives everything, so that's why he's a great artist.[9]

Warhol's own health problems weren't over. In the spring of 1973, shortly after a hectic period when he commuted from New York and Rome during the shooting in Italy of *Andy Warhol's Frankenstein* and *Andy Warhol's Dracula*, he was admitted to hospital with gallstones.

The doctors decided not to operate: instead, they told him to rest and changed his diet.

A Renewed *Interview*

Warhol had been considering closing his magazine, *Interview*, which had gone through multiple editors and lost money instead of making it. But now Fred Hughes suggested instead that they change the magazine's focus. Instead of an underground film magazine written by poets and artists, he said, they should make it "a magazine for people like us!" They eventually settled on Bob Colacello as the editor, and he quickly set the magazine's tone. "We're not interested in journalism so much as taste setting," he said.[10] Of course, Warhol and all his activities were frequently featured.

In February 1974, Warhol's *Mao* paintings opened very successfully in Paris. They were a bigger hit internationally than at home: Warhol didn't even have a New York showing of them. Instead, they were displayed in Cleveland.

In September, Warhol moved the Factory again, though not very far—just across Union Square. The space was set up much more professionally, and all of Warhol's various corporations were now consolidated into Andy Warhol Enterprises. Unlike the high-flying, countercultural 1960s, the 1970s and 1980s would be very business-like.

Warhol's portrait business was booming, headed toward being a million-dollar-a-year operation. Anyone could have a Warhol portrait done for twenty-five thousand dollars. If he thought he could sell more, he'd paint more: the second went for fifteen thousand dollars, the third ten thousand, the fourth five thousand. Collectors often bought these because they were the cheapest Warhols available. In addition to doing portraits of people like Mick Jagger, he began cultivating world leaders as portrait subjects, controversially cozying up to the wives of dictators: Farah Diba, the wife of the Shah of Iran, and Imelda Marcos, wife of the ruler of the Philippines. *Interview* editor Bob Colacello praised the women in his magazine.

Warhol worked hard, several hours a day, seven days a week, then went to parties in the evening. His social circle included people like the fashion designer Halston, author Truman Capote, Bianca Jagger, and actress Liza Minnelli.

Always looking for new worlds to conquer, Warhol had Paul Morrissey working on Warhol's first Broadway musical—although he didn't put up any money for the project, which had music by John Phillips, former leader of the pop group the Mamas and the Papas. Toward the end of rehearsals Morrissey's heavy drug use got him banned from the theater. The show opened on January 29, 1975, and closed three days later. Morrissey never worked with Warhol again. Another of Warhol's former actors, Eric Emerson, who had starred in *Chelsea Girls*, died that May of a heroin overdose.

Thanks to Colacello's connections with the wife of the Shah of Iran, Warhol realized a lifelong dream on May 15, 1975, when he was invited to the White House. The occasion was a state dinner with the Shah.

That September, Warhol's book *The Philosophy of Andy Warhol,* full of his observations on love, fame, beauty and money, was published. His short version of his philosophy: "Everything is nothing." He also liked to say that the most exciting thing about making anything was "not doing it."[11]

According to Bob Colacello, Warhol's "not doing it" philosophy extended to the writing of his book. Colacello said he mostly wrote four chapters, Pat Hackett wrote nine, Brigid Berlin wrote one, and all three of them worked on the prologue. When he saw Warhol photographed for the cover of *New York* magazine, sitting at a typewriter, Colacello said, "It finally hit me then—I was part of a big lie and while it had lined my pockets, it robbed my ego of any hope of recognition."[12]

At the end of the month, Warhol moved into a six-story mansion. It was the first time he had had a place entirely to himself, and he would live there until he died. Warhol's passion for collecting, now given free rein, turned into an obsession. By the time he died, most of the rooms would be completely full of stuff—everything from the cheapest junk to expensive rugs, jewelry, and furniture.

Warhol's Last Film

In 1976, Warhol filmed *Bad.* It was supposed to be low-budget, but it ended up costing more than $1.2 million. Warhol refused to put any money into it. In order to save the project, Fred Hughes invested two hundred thousand dollars, his entire life's savings. It was the

Warhol stands in front of the portrait painted by Jamie Wyeth.

only 1970s Warhol film not directed by Paul Morrissey; instead that task fell to Jed Johnson. Pat Hackett provided the script. Carroll Baker starred as a woman who ran an electrolysis business during the day and at night sent out an all-girl hit squad to commit crimes for her clients.

The movie flopped, and Warhol never made another film. Instead, he showed a renewed focus on art. He collaborated with artist Jamie Wyeth, son of the famous painter Andrew Wyeth: they were commissioned to paint each other's portraits and show the results, along with their initial drawings, at the Coe-Kerr Gallery in Manhattan. The show was a success.

In 1977, Warhol's first major New York show since the *Silver Pillows* show back in 1966 opened in Leo Castelli's gallery. The paintings, some of the largest Warhol had done since the *Mao* portraits, featured the hammer and sickle—the symbols of Communism—but not arranged as they were on the flag of the Soviet Union.

And, of course, the profitable portraits continued, including one in 1976 of Democratic presidential candidate (and soon-to-be-President) Jimmy Carter. Then, in 1977, something new arrived on the New York social scene and in Warhol's life: a club called Studio 54.

Chapter 7

The Final Years

Studio 54 was the creation of Steve Rubell and Ian
Schraeger, and it immediately became *the* place to be
seen in New York—assuming you were rich, powerful,
beautiful, or famous enough to get in. The club's
central decorating feature was also a pretty good
indication of what went on there. It was a neon sign of
the Man in the Moon, which dropped from the ceiling
and sniffed cocaine, represented by twinkling lights,
up its nose.

Everyone around Warhol was taking drugs, although
he was never seen sniffing cocaine. Warhol was
fascinated by Studio 54. It became almost a second
office for him, a place where he found new people to
work at the Factory, to paint, or to interview for
Interview. The magazine had become a great success
partially because it was like Studio 54 in print: a place
to be seen just for the sake of being seen.

According to Jed Johnson, the opening of Studio 54
coincided with a change in Warhol. "That was New York

when it was at the height of its most decadent period. . . .
Andy was just wasting his time, and it was really
upsetting. . . . He just spent his time with the most
ridiculous people."[1] As had become his custom
everywhere, Warhol tape-recorded everything and
took a lot of photographs.

Musically, the era was divided between punk and
disco. Punks claimed Warhol for their own when he
went to Europe for the opening of his *Hammer and
Sickle Show* in Paris, but thanks to Studio 54, he will
always be associated with disco. Nevertheless, he
dipped his toe into the music world again by managing
his own punk-rock act, Walter Steding, who also worked
as a painting assistant. He put out a Steding album on
his own music label, Earhol, but it failed to sell. Steding
was eventually fired as an assistant by Warhol (who
rarely fired anyone) when he was several hours late
turning up for work one day.

In June 1977, Warhol visited the White House
again for a special reception honoring artists who had
contributed prints to the Carter campaign. He was
particularly friendly with the president's mother, Miss
Lillian, and even took her to Studio 54 one night, along
with actress Lucie Arnaz.

Profitable Portraits

Portraits continued to be Warhol's most profitable line of
business. He painted a series called *Athletes*, which
featured Kareem Abdul Jabar, Muhammad Ali, Chris
Evert, Dorothy Hamill, Jack Nicklaus, Pele, Tom Seaver,
Willie Shoemaker, and O.J. Simpson. The sale of these

paintings and prints eventually brought in a million dollars.

Despite the nightly parties, not just at Studio 54—Warhol once said he'd go to the opening of anything, even a toilet seat—he turned out an enormous number of paintings during this period. Most of this work was not shown in the United States. Among the paintings was the *Oxidation* series, created by people urinating on canvases coated with wet copper paint. The paint oxidized and turned orange and green where the urine hit it. The paintings were a hit in Europe, even though they smelled faintly of their featured ingredient.

But the business-like atmosphere that had prevailed for several years at the new Factory was beginning to fall apart under the late-70s onslaught of drugs and alcohol. Warhol's reaction to the problems of those around him was contradictory, says Bockris, "a mixture of genuine concern and tacit encouragement." According to Ronnie Cutrone, "Andy was what they call in AA (Alcoholics Anonymous) a para-alcoholic . . . attracted unconsciously to people with compulsive problems."[2]

Warhol finally had another New York opening in January 1979, when *Shadows*, a series of massive paintings based on photographs of shadows, opened at the Heiner Freidrich Gallery. They sold out before the show even opened.

Warhol Turns Fifty

That August Warhol celebrated his fiftieth birthday at Studio 54. The designer Halston hosted the party. The presents included a pair of roller skates, a garbage pail full of one-dollar bills which were dumped over his head, and five thousand free Studio 54 drink tickets.

Grosset and Dunlap, a New York publishing house, shortly afterward announced the launch of Andy Warhol Books. The first book from the new imprint would be a collection of his photos of celebrities, called *Andy Warhol's Exposures*. It would be followed by a memoir of the 1960s called *POPism*, written with Pat Hackett. Sales of *Exposure*, as was true of most of Warhol's books, proved to be disappointing.

Warhol also made a move into television in 1978, producing a cable television program called *Andy Warhol's TV*, a weekly half-hour of conversations, fashion shows, and visits to celebrity homes. Warhol continued to produce cable TV shows until his death, with limited success.

On November 19, 1979, a huge collection of fifty-six of the portraits that had paid the bills throughout the decade were exhibited at the Whitney Museum. Some of the subjects, such as Sylvester Stallone and Truman Capote, were at the celebrity-studded opening.

Critical remarks about the show seemed to be aimed at Warhol as much as at the art. "The faces are ugly and a shade stoned, if not actually repulsive and grotesque," wrote the *New York Times* critic, who called the work "shallow and boring" and commented on "the debased and brutalized feeling that characterizes every element of this style. That this . . . may be deliberate does not alter the offense."[3] This showed, as critic Peter

Schjeldahl wrote, "Warhol has, once again, hit some kind of nerve."[4]

Over at Studio 54, meanwhile, the party was ending. In January, owners Steve Rubell and Ian Schrager were sentenced to three and a half years in prison and fined twenty thousand dollars each for tax evasion. One of the triggers for the bust by the Internal Revenue Service was a *New York* magazine cover in November that listed Studio 54's "Party Favors," including drugs for various celebrities and "$800 for Andy Warhol's Garbage Pail on his Birthday."[5]

Looking Backward

As seemed to be the case more often than not, various Warhol associates were having serious personal struggles. And Warhol was once again alienating the people around him, including Fred Hughes and Bob Colacello.

Maybe that was why his first art project of the 1980s was called *Reversals*. In it, he took some of his best-known paintings from the 1960s and early 1970s and made negatives of them so they largely looked black, as if they were in mourning.

After that, he revisited his own work again in *Retrospectives*, an assortment of his most famous images on giant canvases. He continued his backward glances in April 1980, when his memoir *POPism* was published. It gained little positive attention.

Jed Johnson moved out of Warhol's house in 1980, leaving Warhol depressed. He redoubled his efforts to cram the house full of stuff, going on regular shopping expeditions to flea markets.

Warhol also decided to take better care of himself. He gave up drinking, started eating health food, and worked out every day with a personal trainer.

The shooting in 1968 still weighed on him. In a 1981 interview, he told a German reporter that "I'm afraid. I'm nervous . . . by chance I opened a letter in which it said, 'Live or die,' and yesterday the letter writer called me. We called the police but they can't do anything until you're killed."[6]

He cheered up, though, when he fell in love with thirty-year-old Jon Gould, who moved in with him in 1983. Although Gould was never seen in public as Warhol's companion, according to friends the relationship bolstered Warhol's spirits. "Jon was a light inside his life," said one.[7]

Other relationships, however, continued to fall apart, among them the one with Bob Colacello, editor of *Interview*. Warhol seemed to feel Colacello was trying to take over. The final straw came when Colacello demanded ownership of *Interview*. Warhol turned him down. Colacello left the Factory for good in February 1983.

On the other hand, Warhol was cultivating new relationships among a new generation of New York artists, who were working in a suddenly booming art marketplace. Two groups in particular were attracted to him. One was the neo-expressionists, whose work featured strong brushstrokes, contrasting colors, and distorted subjects. Their paintings were typically large, sometimes featured found objects, and were created quickly.

The other group was made up of "graffiti" artists, of whom the best known was Jean-Michel Basquiat. Born in 1960 in Brooklyn, Basquiat was the son of a Haitian-American father and a Puerto Rican mother. He'd shown a talent for drawing at a young age, and gained notoriety as a graffiti artist before moving into fine art. In 1981 he was part of a group show at a gallery on Long Island. Dealers and critics were impressed with his work.

Warhol met him in 1979, but despite Basquiat's talent, for a long time Warhol wouldn't let him into the Factory, perhaps because of his reputation for being unpredictable—and a drug user.

Warhol, meanwhile, was churning out more portrait series: *Ten Portraits of Jews of the Twentieth Century*—they sold for three hundred thousand dollars each—and a series of American mythical figures, including Superman, Mickey Mouse, and Uncle Sam. He also did a New York show of dollar signs: not a single painting sold.

Fortunately, *Dollar Signs* was much more appreciated in Paris. Warhol always seemed to do better in Europe. A show of paintings of German monuments did well in Berlin, and his *Guns, Knives and Crosses* show, which featured images of the gun Valerie Solanas shot him with, sold out in Madrid, where one wealthy woman bought the whole lot.

Even if Warhol wasn't doing the most groundbreaking work of his career, his pieces rapidly appreciated in value. In 1983, two of his paintings, *Dick Tracy* and *Saturday's Popeye*, both from 1961, sold for more than a million dollars each. A series of paintings of animals from endangered species, shown at the Museum of Natural History, earned him another million or more. His work was now seen as a solid investment.

The Final Factory

Warhol needed the money from art sales. He'd decided to move the Factory again, and this time he bought an entire building: a five-story disused electrical generator station that stretched from 32nd to 33rd Street between Madison and Fifth Avenues. It would have to be completely renovated—an expensive project that eventually cost $3 million—and the sale price alone was $2 million.

Fortunately, other enterprises were also looking up. *Interview* continued to make a profit, and Warhol was appearing in advertisements for a variety of products, getting paid up to ten thousand dollars for a photo shoot. His wealth was conservatively estimated at $20 million, and he was generating between $3 million and $5 million in revenue a year, two-thirds of that from art.

In 1983, Warhol's Swiss art dealer, Bruno Bischofberger, put up money for a series of three-way collaborations among Warhol, Jean-Michel Basquiat (whose paintings were selling for ten thousand to twenty thousand dollars at that time), and another artist, Francesco Clemente. Warhol lifted the Basquiat ban at the Factory.

118

"Warhol's contribution to these works consisted primarily of handpainted corporate logos and newspaper headlines to which Basquiat added his typical primitivistic drawings of faces and silhouetted figures," says biographer David Bourdon.[8]

The resulting works weren't received as enthusiastically as Bischofberger had hoped, but Warhol and Basquiat had hit it off. Basquiat stayed at the Factory to work on more paintings with Warhol. In a unique collaborative process, they would pass the canvases back and forth, each adding new elements each time. "In the end they looked like a succession of brilliant defacements of each other's work," says Victor Bockris.[9] In one of them, *Brown Spots*, Basquiat portrayed Warhol as a banana. In another, Warhol portrayed Basquiat as Michelangelo's *David*—except this David wore a jockstrap.

Basquiat claimed he helped Warhol more than Warhol helped him. "Andy hadn't painted for years when we met," he said. "He was very disillusioned."[10] Warhol's friends were a bit surprised by the friendship between the two, not least because of Basquiat's drug use, something Warhol no longer tolerated. According to Bourdon, after Basquiat moved into a two-story building owned by Warhol that rented for four thousand dollars a month, Basquiat often paid his rent late, "partly because he was extravagant with money and also because he had developed a $1,000 a week cocaine habit."[11]

Other new young artists of the 1980s also seemed to have an affinity for Warhol, who in turn seemed to have an affinity for them. After all, he'd done the whole

In 1985, Warhol and Jean-Michel Basquiat pose in front of their paintings.

avant-garde thing long before they arrived on the scene: it made him a kind of aging role model.

Warhol's interest in trying to keep healthy led him to a chiropractor in 1984, who had a non-chiropractic sideline: he believed wearing crystals could promote good health by tapping into "healing energy" and "vibrations." Warhol took to wearing a crystal pendant around his neck. He continued to exercise. He also went to a dermatologist for collagen shots to try to keep his face wrinkle-free. He went to his own doctor every week. He may have hated hospitals, but he loved doctors. "He was seeking the fountain of youth," said the chiropractor, Dr. Andrew Bernsohn.[12]

Warhol made his biggest public appearance on October 12, 1985: he appeared as himself in an episode of the TV show *The Love Boat*. It helped change his image in the parts of America where he'd been seen as little more than some kind of New York freak. At the same time, critics—possibly propelled by the interest the hot new artists had in Warhol—were beginning to think that maybe he was more important as an artist than they'd generally believed.

The Factory moved for the last time into the new building Warhol had bought in December 1984. The huge structure had three separate wings, each with its own entrance. The Factory occupied one, *Interview* occupied another, and the third was rented out. It had a ballroom-sized space in which Warhol could paint, a video studio, a screening room, expanded offices, two kitchens, and other facilities, but what Warhol really liked about it was all the storage space it offered. "Hundreds of paintings could be stored, along with prints, unfinished projects . . . and most importantly, his own acquisitions. . . . What didn't make it up to his house on East 66th Street ended up at the office."[13]

Deteriorating Relationships

As often happened with Warhol, though, advances in his career were counterbalanced by problems in his personal life. His boyfriend Jon Gould was diagnosed with AIDS, which had already claimed several of

Warhol's more distant friends and an editor of *Interview*, Robert Hayes. Even though Warhol hated hospitals, when Gould spent several weeks in New York Hospital in 1985, Warhol visited him every day, sometimes staying for hours.

After he got out of the hospital, Gould left Warhol's house and moved to Los Angeles. Warhol felt betrayed, and soon refused to talk about him. Gould died in September 1986.

Meanwhile, Warhol's relationship with Basquiat was also deteriorating. Basquiat wasn't handling his success well. After he read something in *The New York Times* suggesting he was too influenced by Warhol, Basquiat stopped talking to him and quit paying him rent. When their joint show opened in September 1985, neither man spoke to each other, and Basquiat didn't attend the opening night dinner party. Basquiat would outlive Warhol, but not by much: he died of an overdose of heroin and cocaine in 1988.

Warhol also wasn't getting along with Fred Hughes. The tension between them infected the whole staff, none of whom really liked each other very much. "Andy did not live in a pleasant world," wrote Bockris. "Most of the people he saw would have killed each other for money, glamour and fame if it had not been against the law. They were sarcastic, scornful and contemptuous."[14]

Still, Warhol kept drawing new people to him—or going to them. He loved hanging out with rock stars like Madonna, Grace Jones, and Sting. He was a guest at the wedding of Maria Shriver and Arnold Schwarzenegger.

He continued to work hard on commissions from all over the world. But to his associates, despite his frantic pace, he seemed lonely and depressed.

What they didn't know was that he was already feeling ill. The gallstones that had given him a painful attack in 1973 were acting up again. He spent a lot of time thinking and talking about the past, and a lot of time alone in his house with only his two maids for company.

"I don't think Uncle Andy was very happy at all," said his nephew George Warhola, who worked at the Factory for a time but left in 1985. "All that money and fame didn't make him happy."[15]

Final Works

In the summer of 1986 Warhol painted a series of self-portraits, based on a photograph with his wig sticking up at wild angles. John Caldwell bought one for the Carnegie Museum in Philadelphia, where, as a child, Warhol had taken art lessons. Caldwell later wrote, "He looks simultaneously ravaged and demonic, blank and full of too many years and too much experience."[16]

The portraits were well-received when they were shown in London in July. Warhol seemed a bit happier when he returned. Various other enterprises continued to go well. Warhol had found a new outlet for his film and television aspirations, directing music videos for bands like the Cars, and making cameo appearances in some of them. *Interview* continued to prosper.

That same year, Warhol created a series of *Camouflage* paintings. He modeled them after a swatch of camouflage netting he'd bought at an army surplus store. He would give the canvas an overall coat of the lightest color, then paint the three darker colors over it. In addition to using normal camouflage shades of green, brown and gray, he used reds and pinks. Some of the paintings consisted only of camouflage patterns, but on some he superimposed portraits, including his own.

According to Thomas Sokolowski, curator of the Warhol Museum, these late paintings of camouflage actually lie at the heart of all of Warhol's work:

> [T]his notion of presenting something as his own person or art that was very specifically and jointly constructed, to create a kind of everyman who would respond to the world and on behalf of the world to create images that would allow us to see ourselves perhaps more accurately, perhaps more efficiently than we had in the past.

In his view, this idea of camouflage, of things hidden beneath the surface, permeates everything Warhol did, from the early pop art paintings to the portraits of famous people to, especially, his own life.

"Camouflage came from something that was supposed to dazzle your eyes so you would not see or countenance what was under that camouflage," Sokolowski says. "That notion of dazzling was something he was playing with. What (Warhol) seems to do seems so hapless, so nonchalent, so easy to do. Art is supposed to be about struggle. That's not part of Warhol's idea at all." Instead, he says, Warhol had "the Italian idea that a courtier should be able to do something that was very difficult, but it should look like there was no effort whatsoever."[17]

In the latter part of 1986, Warhol finished a series of paintings based on Leonardo da Vinci's *The Last Supper*, commissioned by his first New York dealer, Alexander Iolas, who had closed his gallery in Manhatten and moved permanently to Europe. Iolas planned to show the works in Milan, in a gallery right across a street from the church which houses the original. Some of the paintings were done by hand, others were silkscreened. In the end, he chose only to show the silkscreened ones.

During the same time frame, Warhol did portraits of Vladimir Lenin, head of the Soviet Union in the mid-1900s. It looked like 1987 would be a huge year

Andy Warhol, in 1986, in front of one of his self portraits.

for Warhol, and indeed it started well, with a collection of his photographs, hand-stitched in multiples of four to twelve, opening in January to the best reviews he'd had in New York in years.

Two weeks later he flew to Milan for the opening of his *Last Supper* paintings. It would prove to be the last show of his work during his lifetime.

The Death of Andy Warhol

The pain from his gallstones was continuing to plague Warhol. It was a sign of how much the pain was bothering him when he decided to stay home instead of going out on the night of February 13, because Warhol always went out. The next day he complained to his dermatologist; she scheduled an ultrasound that showed his gallbladder was enlarged. On Monday, February 16, he canceled all his appointments. Tuesday he appeared with jazz trumpeter Miles Davis in a fashion show; a photograph of the two of them together is one of the final ones taken of Warhol. He was obviously in terrible pain.

On February 18, Warhol visited his regular doctor, who diagnosed an acutely infected gallbladder that needed to be removed right away. Warhol wanted to put it off for a few more days, but a second ultrasound showed the gallbladder to be severely inflamed and filled with fluid.

The plan was for Warhol to have the operation on Saturday and be home by Sunday. No one but his closest aides knew. He checked in to New York Hospital under an assumed name, Bob Robert. The surgery was performed between 8:45 A.M. and 12:10 P.M. on Saturday, February 21, and there were no complications.

After three hours in the recovery room, he was taken to his private room on the twelfth floor, where he was cared for by a private duty nurse. He seemed to be recovering normally when the doctors checked on him in the afternoon and early evening, and at about 9:30 P.M. he phoned his housekeeper.

At 5:45 A.M. the nurse noticed that the sleeping Warhol had turned blue and his pulse had weakened. A cardiac arrest team was unable revive him and he was pronounced dead at 6:31 A.M., apparently from a heart attack. The New York State Department of Health later concluded that "the active medical staff of the hospital did not assure the maintenance of the proper quality of all medication and treatment provided to patient." A wrongful-death suit was brought against the hospital by Warhol's estate, and was settled out of court for $3 million, which went to Warhol's brothers in exchange for an agreement that they would not contest his will.[18]

CNN broke the news of Warhol's death at noon on Sunday. The next day it was on the front pages of newspapers around the world. Warhol's associates, most of whom hadn't even known he was ill, were shocked.

The first to learn of Warhol's death was Fred Hughes. He and his lawyer, Edward Hayes, along with a security guard, arrived at Warhol's house shortly after 7 A.M. They opened the safe and began examining its contents, including the will, which specified that most of his estate was to be set aside to fund the Andy Warhol

Foundation for the Visual Arts. *Interview* and Andy Warhol Enterprises would continue as nonprofit businesses with Fred Hughes as chairman of the board.

Hughes was also to receive $250,000, the same amount Warhol left to both of his brothers, John and Paul. Nobody had thought to notify them: John found out when he called at 11 A.M. for his usual weekly chat with Andy. He called Paul.

It fell to Paul and John to make funeral arrangements. Their mother had wanted Andy to be buried next to her in the St. John the Divine Byzantine Cemetery in Pittsburgh, so a plot was already waiting for him there.

An open-coffin wake was held in Pittsburgh on Wednesday, February 25. Warhol was dressed in a black cashmere suit, a paisley tie, a platinum wig, and his sunglasses. He held a small black prayer book and a red rose. The funeral was to be held the next day, attended mostly by Warhol's relatives and their friends from Pittsburgh. Only a few people from the Factory were present and no celebrities, because Hughes had announced, though the family hadn't asked him to, that the family wanted as few guests as possible.

On February 26, a mass was held at Holy Ghost Byzantine Catholic Church. Following the service, a procession of twenty cars drove twenty-five miles to the cemetery. Another brief service was held in a small chapel near the cemetery entrance, then the mourners followed the hearse to the graveside. A simple marble slab, carved with Warhol's name and the dates of his death and birth, marked the grave into which the bronze coffin was lowered.

The priest said a prayer and sprinkled holy water on Warhol's casket, but the last thing to go into the grave before it was filled in was a copy of *Interview* and a bottle of Warhol's favorite Estée Lauder perfume.[19]

Chapter 8

The Andy Warhol Legacy

More than two decades have passed since Andy Warhol's death, and he continues to be a polarizing figure. People either love him or hate him, but very few are indifferent to him.

One thing that seems obvious is that he's not going away. Major exhibitions of his work continue to be mounted on a regular basis, not only because curators and critics see the work as important, but also because a Warhol show is sure to draw a crowd.

Warhol's immediate legacy, of course, was his enormous estate, estimated conservatively to be worth $200 million at the time of his death but possibly worth as much as $500 million. In his will, Warhol stipulated that the bulk of his wealth should go to create a foundation dedicated to the "advancement of the visual arts."

In accordance with his wishes, the Warhol Foundation was created. Warhol had also stipulated that the directors of the new foundation should be Fred

Hughes, Vincent Fremont, and John Warhola. In 1988, Fred Hughes hired Archibald Gillies as a consultant to the Foundation. Gillies became president in March 1990.

Hughes resigned from the Foundation on February 11, 1992. He'd been critical of the Foundation in the press, and the board told him if he didn't resign, he'd be voted out.[1]

Gillies remained president until October 2001, at which time he was succeeded by Joel Wachs, who had previously served on the Los Angeles City Council and was already recognized nationally as a champion of the arts.

During Gillies' twelve years as president, the Foundation converted the art bequeathed to it by Warhol into more than $131 million in cash and investment, while distributing more than $41 million in 1,190 cash grants to help advance the visual arts.

Warhol's fortune, through the Warhol Foundation, has also helped establish Creative Capital, a foundation to support individual artists. In its first five years, Creative Capital helped more than one hundred fifty artists with cash grants and career development advice. The Warhol Foundation recently gave Creative Capital an additional ten-year, $10-million gift to continue its work.

In its first five years, another Foundation project, the Warhol Initiative, provided substantial support to thirty-one small- to mid-sized artist-based organizations, helping them achieve greater financial security so they can continue their services to artists and art audiences.

Warhol's Artistic Legacy

Another focus of the Foundation has been to strengthen and enhance Andy Warhol's artistic—as opposed to financial—legacy. To that end, in 1994 the Foundation founded the Andy Warhol Museum in Warhol's hometown of Pittsburgh, getting it started with a donation of more than thirty-nine hundred works of art—not just paintings, but also drawings, photographs, prints, film and video, sculpture, and archival material from the Warhol estate.

The Foundation funded the preservation of all of Warhol's film and video work at the Museum of Modern

Warhol the Packrat

Among the archival material donated to the Warhol Museum by the Warhol Foundation were Warhol's Time Capsules: a series of boxes which, from 1974 onwards, he filled monthly with whatever happened to be on his bedroom dresser at the time.

The Warhol Museum is only a fifth of the way through opening those six hundred boxes, according to Thomas Sokolowski, the museum's director, and so far they've found "bills, pornography, letters . . . a painting worth half a million, a petrified foot, [and] fifteen thousand dollars in cash."[2]

"He was a packrat who never threw anything away," says Sokolowski, who points out that in 1988 the sale of the stuff Warhol had squirreled away in his house from his daily buying trips took seven days of sales at Sotheby's, four or five hours a day. The final take was $29 million. Among the big sellers: 185 cookie jars, perfectly ordinary except for having been originally purchased by Warhol. They netted $187,000—a little over $1,000 apiece.

Art in New York. In March 2002, it published to critical acclaim the *Andy Warhol Catalogue Raisonné Vol. I: Painting and Sculpture 1961-63*. Volume 2, covering the Factory years from 1964 to 1969, was published in 2004, and work is continuing on subsequent volumens.

In October 2003, the Foundation funded a symposium and film series at the Brooklyn Academy of Music to mark the 75th anniversary of Warhol's birth. And, the Foundation makes the collection available for exhibitions worldwide, and usually several of these are going on at any given time.

Even while he was alive Warhol made a concerted effort to market not only his art but also his name. He appeared in ads and lent his name to various projects, though he seldom put money into them.

The Warhol Foundation is following in his footsteps. Licensed products designed from Warhol images have appeared in numerous lifestyle magazines and were featured in the popular HBO series *Sex and the City*. There's a whole line of Andy Warhol products—clothing, housewares, and stationery—which is already well-established and successful in Europe, where Warhol's art was frequently accepted more readily than in the United States when he was alive.

Warhol's Artistic Importance

But Warhol's real legacy isn't his fortune, but the art itself. There's a lot of it: he created some thirty-two thousand paintings and prints during his lifetime.[3] Shortly after his death, critics began to look at his life's work with fresh eyes. Although by "hitching his wagon"

Even today, people flock to Andy Warhol exhibits. This exhibit opened in 2008 at the Montreal Museum of Fine Arts in Canada.

to stars like Marilyn Monroe and Elvis Presley and using pop-culture references like Campbell's Soup cans in his work, Warhol made himself into a kind of "mythic figure and cultural emblem of his times," says biographer David Bourdon. "Warhol was also a gifted artist. . . . Bucking the prevailing trend of painterly abstraction, he injected new freshness and vitality in some of the most traditional categories of painting—portraits, still lifes, and genre."[4] His willingness to use anything and everything from the mass media in his work has expanded the range of subject matter available to painters.

But beyond that, Bourdon suggests, Warhol pioneered two major artistic innovations that will insure his importance in art history. The first is his unique use of repetitions, using representational images to create seemingly abstract grids. "His grid compositions enabled him to 'abstract' his ready-made pictorial subjects and make them comply with the formal requirements of a 'flat' painting style," Bourdon notes.[5]

Warhol's second major innovation was the use of the silkscreen printing method to apply pigment to canvas. This makes it look as though the image has been simply mechanically reproduced, when in fact Warhol's artistic input can be seen in the choice of colors and the imperfections: for example, the way the colors are off-register (not quite lined up with the parts of the image they should appear in).[6]

In his introduction to a Warhol retrospective at the Museum of Modern Art in 1989, the chief curator, Kynaston McShine, described Warhol's position in modern American culture: "He was one of the most serious, and one of the most important, artists of the twentieth century. He quite simply changed how we see all the world around us. He had an uncanny ability to select precise images that still have great resonance today."[7]

"He used art as a means of bringing to the attention of the masses facts and ideas which afterwards seemed so obvious as to make it surprising that so few really saw them," says Klaus Honnef. "Through his contribution art is no longer what it was."[8]

Warhol and Religion

The fact "you can never tell" what Warhol had in mind with a particular work of art contributes to making that art a continuing focus of discussion and reflection. Opinions about the artist and his work can vary widely.

Consider *The Last Supper* paintings, the last ones exhibited while Warhol was alive. In her book *The Religious Art of Andy Warhol*, Jane Daggett Dillenberger notes that Warhol often used religious imagery in his work, and traces that to his upbringing as a Byzantine Catholic. According to Dillenberger, Warhol never lost his faith, "even when it came into conflict with his sexuality and his immersion in the drug-soaked milieu of the New York underground." She envisions him as a kind of closeted Christian and sees *The Last Supper* paintings as "a kind of last will and testament," writing "In these last paintings the formerly cool and distanced artist finally created paintings in which his concealed religiosity flowed freely into his art."[9]

But Cliff Edwards, professor of religious studies at Virginia Commonwealth University in Richmond, Virginia, disagrees. "Warhol did go to church regularly and helped feed the poor three times a year. He honored his parents' piety, a piety that connected going to church with 'getting to heaven.' But he wanted no part of the church's community, its rites of confession or the mass."[10]

He believes Warhol painted *The Last Supper* paintings for the same reason he painted *Campbell Soup* cans: he "was fascinated by any image that caught the public eye, by the iconic commodity value of either a Mickey Mouse, a gun or a cheap replica of Leonardo's *Last Supper*." He notes that Warhol described the opening of his *Last Supper* show in Milan as "scary and stupid."[11]

The debate about the influence of religion on Warhol, as with so many other questions about the artist, his life, and his work, continues.

"Although he never claimed any intellectual significance for his artworks, he knew they were aesthetically innovative and exemplary reflections on the American Dream," writes David Bourdon. "He became a pictorial chronicler of the American way of life, depicting many of the faces, products and events that exemplified his era."[12]

Over the Halloween weekend in 2008, Harvard University hosted a conference entitled "Andy, 80? Considering the Warhol Legacies on His 80th Birthday."

"The spectrum of Warhol's production is broader than any other artist of that whole period and that in and of itself is quite an accomplishment," Buchloh says. "It makes him an absolutely central figure for . . . artists working in the world now in global contexts. The internationalism that Warhol has brought about is stunning."[13]

And, says Helen Molesworth, Curator of Contemporary Art at Harvard's Fogg Museum, Warhol is particularly relevant to today's youth: "I think the current generation . . . exists in a world with more images than any other group of people ever on the history of the planet. . . .Warhol is the artist who has the most to tell us about all those different kinds of images and how they work together."[14]

Warhol Museum director Thomas Sokolowski points out that YouTube is the embodiment of Warhol's most famous quote, "In the future everybody will be world-famous for fifteen minutes," which, he notes, Warhol actually lifted from a "more boring text" by media critic Marshall McLuhan. Warhol saw that coming long before anyone else did, Sokolowski says—and realized the pitfalls: "He understood that with this new fame, this new engagement with the world, we are opening up a Pandora's box."[15]

There is a tendency to think of Warhol as nothing more than a brand name, like the Coke bottles or Campbell's Soup cans he painted. But even as his Foundation markets his name and his images all over the world, more than twenty years after his death, it's becoming more and more obvious that he was far more than that. He is, says Buchloh, an artist whose influence has yet to diminish. He was also, without a doubt, a true American rebel.

Chronology[1]

1928—On August 6, Andrew Warhola is born in Pittsburgh to Julia and Ondrej Warhola.

1936–1937—Andy starts attending free Saturday art classes at the Carnegie Museum; he contracts St. Vitus' dance after a bout of rheumatic fever and is confined to bed for more than two months.

1942—Andy graduates from Holmes Elementary School and enters Schenley High School; his father, Ondrej Warhola, dies after a lengthy illness.

1945—Andy Warhola enrolls in the Department of Painting and Design at the Carnegie Institute of Technology (presently Carnegie Mellon University).

1947–1948—Andy experiments with the blotted-line drawing technique that he will use to great effect as a commercial artist; he works at a summer job in the display department at the Joseph Horne department store; Andy has two paintings in the annual exhibition of the Associated Artists of Pittsburgh.

1949—Andy's painting of a boy picking his nose is rejected for the annual exhibition of the Associated Artists of Pittsburgh; he graduates with a bachelor of fine arts degree in pictorial design; he moves to New York City and begins working as a commercial artist, using the name Andy Warhol.

1952—Warhol's first solo exhibition, *Fifteen Drawings Based on the Writings of Truman Capote*, opens at the Hugo Gallery; Julia Warhola moves to New York to live with Andy.

1953—Begins making his own illustrated books which he gives to clients and associates and sells in shops.

1954—Exhibits work in both group and solo shows at the Loft Gallery in New York City.

1955—Chosen by the shoe company I. Miller to illustrate its weekly newspaper advertisements.

1956—A drawing of a shoe is included in the exhibition *Recent Drawings U.S.A.* at the Museum of Modern Art; goes on a two-month world tour with Charles Lisanby.

1957—Andy Warhol Enterprises is legally incorporated.

1959—With Suzie Frankfurt, self-publishes *Wild Raspberries*, a cookbook of absurd recipes.

1960–1961—Paints his first works based on comics and advertisements; shows several paintings in a Bonwit Teller department store window with a display of dresses.

1962—Begins using photo-silkscreen technique; creates first celebrity portraits, including the Marilyn Monroe paintings; Campbell's Soup

Can paintings are shown at the Ferus Gallery in Los Angeles; featured in a *Time* magazine article on pop artists.

1963–1964—Does first commissioned portrait, of collector Ethel Scull; begins painting Elvis Presley and Elizabeth Taylor paintings; buys his first 8 mm movie camera; makes films *Sleep*, *Kiss*, *Haircut*, and *Tarzan and Jane Regained . . . Sort Of*, and the first of more than five hundred *Screen Tests*; rents an abandoned firehouse near his home for use as a painting studio; studio becomes known as "the Factory"; makes the *Thirteen Most Wanted Men* mural for the facade of the New York Pavilion at the 1964 New York World's Fair, then covers it with silver paint after officials object to it; constructs *Brillo Boxes* and other box sculptures, which are shown at the Stable Gallery; begins series of Jackie Kennedy paintings after President Kennedy's assassination; continues making films, including *Eat*, *Empire*, and *Harlot* (his first film with live sound).

1965—Makes more films, including several with Edie Sedgwick; exhibits video art, the first artist to do so; announces in Paris he is retiring from painting in order to devote himself to film; the opening night crowd at the retrospective of Warhol's work in Philadelphia overwhelms the facility; meets Paul Morrissey.

1966–1967—Produced the *Exploding Plastic Inevitable* multimedia shows featuring the

Velvet Underground; films *Chelsea Girls*, which receives international media attention; produces the first album by the Velvet Underground and Nico and designs the cover with a peelable banana; self-portraits included in the United States Pavilion at Expo '67 in Montreal; films *Bike Boy, I, A Man*, and *Nude Restaurant*; publishes *Screen Tests/A Diary*; goes on a college lecture tour, but has Allen Midgette impersonate him at several universities; meets Frederick W. Hughes.

1968—In January, moves studio; on June 3, Valerie Solanas shoots Warhol; while recuperating, produces *Flesh*, directed by Paul Morrissey, and makes *Blue Movie*; *a: a novel* is published by Grove Press.

1969—Produces the film *Trash*, directed by Paul Morrissey; the first issue of *Interview* magazine is published; Vincent Fremont begins to work with Warhol on video and television projects.

1970—Warhol begins to produce more commissioned portraits; Bob Colacello begins to work for *Interview* and eventually becomes its editor.

1971—Designs the album cover of the Rolling Stones' *Sticky Fingers*; cover is nominated for a Grammy Award; Warhol's play *Pork* is performed in London and New York; his ailing mother moves to Pittsburgh.

1972—Begins paintings of Mao Tse-tung; produces the films *Women in Revolt!* and *Heat*, directed by Paul Morrissey; Julia Warhol dies in Pittsburgh.

1974—Begins assembling Time Capsules; directed by Paul Morrissey; *Mao* is exhibited at the Musée Galliera, Paris.

1978—Makes *Self-Portraits With Skulls, Shadows*, and *Oxidation* paintings.

1979—*Andy Warhol's Exposures*, with photographs by Warhol and text co-written with Bob Colacello, is published by Andy Warhol Books/Grosset and Dunlap.

1980—Develops *Andy Warhol's T.V.*; *POPism: The Warhol '60s*, by Warhol and Pat Hackett, is published by Harcourt Brace Jovanovich.

1983—Warhol, Jean-Michel Basquiat, and Francesco Clemente begin collaborating on paintings; Warhol and Basquiat become close friends and continue working together.

1984—Makes a music video for the Cars' "Hello Again," with Don Munroe, and also appears in it; *Collaborations: Jean-Michel Basquiat, Francesco Clemente, Andy Warhol* is exhibited at the Bruno Bischofberger Gallery, Zurich; Warhol moves his operations to a former power generator building.

1985—*America*, with photographs and text by Warhol, is published by Harper and Row;

appears as a guest star in the two hundredth episode of *The Love Boat*.

1986—Makes *Last Supper* and *Camouflage* paintings; makes *Self-Portrait* paintings, which are shown in London.

1987—After several days of acute pain, Warhol enters New York Hospital for gallbladder surgery; dies in hospital of a heart attack on February 22; buried near his parents in Pittsburgh.

Glossary

agent—An artist's business representative, who negotiates contracts and collects money.

amphetamine—A drug that stimulates the central nervous system.

art critic—A person who describes, analyzes, and evaluates artworks, usually for a newspaper, magazine, or other publication.

avant-garde—French for "vanguard"; artists who are innovative or experimental, and whose work is ahead of its time.

barbiturate—A drug that depresses the central nervous system, sometimes used to promote sleep.

cocaine—An addictive drug that produces a feeling of euphoria.

collage—A picture or design created by adhering items such as newspaper clippings, photographs, or cloth to a flat surface.

commercial art—The creation of images or objects for commercial and advertising purposes.

counterculture—A culture with values that run counter to those of established society.

curator—In art, a person who is responsible for collecting, caring for, researching, showing, and writing about an exhibition.

disco—A form of dance music, popular in the 1970s that featured hypnotic rhythm, repetitive lyrics, and electronically produced sounds.

entourage—A group of attendants and associates.

fine art—Art created for its own sake, as opposed to being created for commercial purposes.

gallery—A place for displaying and selling art.

one-man show—An exhibition of art that has all been created by the same person.

portfolio—A collection of pieces that an artist uses to show prospective clients the kind of work he or she is capable of.

punk rock—Rock music that features extreme and often deliberately offensive expressions of social discontent.

realism—Art that realistically depicts people, places, or things.

retrospective—An exhibit that covers the body of work of a particular artist or group of artists.

underground film—A film set apart by its style, genre, or financing that is typically not shown in mainstream movie theaters.

Chapter Notes

Introduction

1. Victor Bockris, *Warhol* (New York: Da Capo Press, 1997), p. 149.
2. "The Slice-of Cake School," *Time*, Friday, May 11, 1962, <http://www.time.com/time/magazine/article/0,9171,939397,00.html> (November 5, 2008).
3. Justin Kaplan, ed., *Bartlett's Familiar Quotations*, 16th Ed. (New York: Little, Brown & Co., 1992), p. 758.
4. Carol Vogel, "Modern Acquires 2 Icons Of Pop Art," *The New York Times*, October 10, 1996, sec. C, p. 19.

Chapter 1. Early Days

1. Victor Bockris, *Warhol* (New York: Da Capo Press, 1997), p. 15.
2. Fred Lawrence Guiles, *Loner at the Ball: The Life of Andy Warhol* (New York: Bantam Press, 1989), p. 12.
3. "Chronology by Year: 1931," *Historic Pittsburgh*, <http://digital.library.pitt.edu/cgi-bin/chronology/chronology_driver.pl?searchtype=ybrowse&year=1931&start_line=0> (June 4, 2009).
4. Bockris, p. 24.
5. "Julia Warhola - Andy Warhol's Mother," *The Andy Warhol Family Album*, n.d., <http://www.warhola.com/andysmother.html> (November 5, 2008).
6. Bockris, p. 33.

7. Ibid., p. 35.

8. Pat Hackett and Andy Warhol, *POPism: The Warhol Sixties* (New York: Harcourt Brace Jovanovich, 1980), p. 109.

9. Bockris, p. 41.

Chapter 2. The Start of the Art

1. Fred Lawrence Guiles, *Loner at the Ball: The Life of Andy Warhol* (New York: Bantam Press, 1989), p. 18.

2. Ellen S. Wilson, "For Depth of Museum Experience, Carnegie Museum of Arts Student Program is Unparalleled," *Carnegie Magazine*, July/August 2001, <http://findarticles.com/p/articles/mi_qa3966/is_/ai_n8958211> (November 6, 2008).

3. Victor Bockris, *Warhol* (New York: Da Capo Press, 1997), pp. 50-51.

4. Ibid., p. 53.

5. Ibid.

6. Andy Warhol, *America* (New York: HarperCollins Children's Books, 1985), p. 8.

7. Bockris, p. 55.

8. Ibid., p. 56.

9. Seth Johnson, "From the Bauhaus to the 21st Century," n.d., <http://web.utk.edu/~art/faculty/kennedy/bauhaus/index.html> (November 6, 2008).

10. "Blotted Line Drawing," *The Warhol: Resources and Lessons*, n.d. <http://edu.warhol.org/aract_blot.html> (November 6, 2008).

11. Jess Kornbluth, *Pre-Pop Warhol* (New York: Panache Press, 1988), p. 10.

12. Bockris, p. 77.

13. "Abstract Expressionism," *ArtLex*, n.d., <http://www.artlex.com/ArtLex/a/abstractexpr.html> (November 7, 2008).
14. Bockris, p. 81.
15. Ibid., p. 86.
16. Ibid., p. 91.
17. David Bourdon, *Warhol* (New York: Harry N. Abrams, Inc., 1989), p. 32.
18. Guiles, p. 95.
19. John Coplans, et al., *Andy Warhol* (New York: Little, Brown & Co., 1970).
20. Bourdon, pp. 36, 37-38.
21. Bockris, p. 107.
22. "The Wig," *Warhol Stars: Serendipity*, n.d., <http://www.warholstars.org/warhol1/5serendipity.html> (November 7, 2008).
23. Bockris, p. 115.
24. Patrick S. Smith, *Andy Warhol's Art and Films* (Ann Arbor: UMI Research Press, 1986), p. 372.
25. Bockris, p. 125.
26. "Doyle News," Doyle New York Website, n.d., <http://www.doylenewyork.com/pr/modern/08PT01/default.htm> (June 5, 2009).
27. "Robert Rauschenberg - About the Artist," *American Masters* Website, n.d., <http://www.pbs.org/wnet/americanmasters/episodes/robert-rauschenberg/about-the-artist/49/> (June 5, 2009).
28. "Jasper Johns - About the Painter," *American Masters Website*, n.d., <http://www.pbs.org/wnet/americanmasters/episodes/jasper-johns/about-the-painter/54/> (June 5, 2009).
29. Ibid.
30. Bourdon, p. 65.

31. Jess Kornbluth, *Pre-Pop Warhol* (New York: Panache Press, 1988), pp. 17–18.

32. Helen Gardner, *Art Through the Ages* (Sixth Edition) (New York: Harcourt Brace Javanovich, 1975), pp. 782–784.

33. Bockris, p. 136.

34. Ibid., p. 142.

35. Ibid., p. 143.

36. Gary Comenas, "The Origin of Andy Warhol's Soup Cans," *Warholstars*, n.d., <http://www.warholstars.org/art/Warhol/soup.html> (November 8, 2008).

Chapter 3. Pop Goes the Factory

1. "Andy Warhol's Methods and Techniques," The Andy Warhol Museum, n.d., <http://www.warhol.org/education/pdfs/methods_and_techs.pdf> (November 8, 2008).

2. Patrick S. Smith, *Andy Warhol's Art and Films* (Ann Arbor: UMI Research Press, 1981), pp. 504–505.

3. Michael Fried, "New York Letter," *Art International*, December 20, 1962.

4. Victor Bockris, *Warhol* (New York: Da Capo Press, 1997), p. 156.

5. Ibid., p. 157.

6. "Pop Art: Cult of the Commonplace," *TIME Magazine*, May 3, 1963, <http://www.time.com/time/magazine/article/0,9171,828186-1,00.html> (June 5, 2009).

7. Paul Greenhalgh, *Quotations and sources on design and the decorative arts* (New York: Manchester University Press, 1993), p. 53.

8. Bockris, p. 187

9. Andy Warhol and Pat Hackett, *POPism: The Warhol Sixties* (New York: Harcourt Brace, 1980), p. 73.

10. David Bourdon, *Warhol* (New York: Harry N. Abrams, Inc., 1989), p. 181.

11. Warhol and Hackett, pp. 71-72.

12. Bourdon, p. 186.

13. David Bourdon, "Andy Warhol and the American Dream," *Andy Warhol: 1928-1987*, (Munich: Prestel-Verlag, 1993), p. 10.

14. Norman Webster, "What is art? Ask Canadian Customs inspectors," *The Montreal Gazette*, November 9, 2008.

15. Bockris, p. 224.

16. John O'Connor and Benjamin Liu, *Unseen Warhol* (New York: Rizzoli, 1996), p. 59.

Chapter 4. **Warhol the Filmmaker**

1. Victor Bockris, *Warhol* (New York: Da Capo Press, 1997), p. 176.

2. Lavanya Ramanathan, "'Sleep': Warhol's 5-Hour Fever Dream," *Washington Post*, April 3, 2008, p. C13.

3. John Giorno, "My 15 Minutes," *The Guardian* (London), February 14, 2002.

4. Jonas Mekas, "Andy Warhol's Sleep," *From Movies*, edited by Gilbert Adair, n.d., <http://beebo.org/smackerels/sleep.html> (November 9, 2008).

5. Andy Warhol, and Pat Hackett, *POPism: The Warhol Sixties* (New York: Harcourt Brace, 1980), p. 32.

6. Bockris, p. 191.

7. Klaus Honnef, *Andy Warhol 1928-1987: Commerce into Art* (Koln, Germany: Benedikt Taschen Verlag, 1993), pp. 79–80.

8. Bockris, p. 207.

9. Gary Indiana, "Mary Woronov," Interview, June-July, 2008.

10. Jean Stein with George Plimpton, *Edie, An American Biography* (New York: Alfred A. Knopf, 1982), p. 234.

11. Douglas Crimp, "Coming Together to Stay Apart," *Warholstars*, n.d., <http://www.warholstars.org/tavel_crimp.html> (June 5, 2009).

12. Bockris, p. 280.

13. David Bourdon, *Warhol* (New York: Harry N. Abrams, Inc., 1989), p. 216.

14. Victor Bockris, *Lou Reed: The Biography* (London: Vintage, 1995), p. 113.

15. Isabell Collin Dufresne (Ultra Violet), *Famous for 15 Minutes: My Years with Andy Warhol* (New York: Harcourt Brace Jovanovich, 1988), p. 169.

Chapter 5. The Shooting of Andy Warhol

1. Bob Colacello, *Holy Terror: Andy Warhol Close Up* (New York: Harper Collins, 1990), p. 32.

2. Victor Bockris, *Warhol* (New York: Da Capo Press, 1997), p. 275.

3. Ibid., p. 278.

4. Robert Hughes, "The Rise of Andy Warhol." *New York Review of Books*, vol. 29, no. 2, 1982.

5. Bockris, p. 283.

6. Andy Warhol and Pat Hackett, *POPism: The Warhol Sixties* (New York: Harcourt Brace, 1980), p. 265.

7. Robert Marmorstein, "SCUM Goddess: A Winter Memory of Valerie Solanis," *Village Voice*, June 13, 1968, p. 9-10, 20.

8. David Bourdon, *Warhol* (New York: Harry N. Abrams, Inc., 1989), p. 284.

9. Ibid.

10. Bockris, p. 301–302.

11. Ibid., p. 303.

12. Bourdon, p. 286.

13. Isabelle Collin Dufresne (Ultra Violet), *Famous for 15 Minutes: My Years with Andy Warhol* (New York: Harcourt Brace Jovanovich, 1988), p. 178.

14. "Felled by Scum," *TIME Magazine*, Friday, June 14, 1968, <http://www.time.com/time/magazine/article/0,9171,900118,00.html> (November 10, 2008).

15. Bockris, p. 324.

16. Ibid., p. 311.

Chapter 6. A Quieter Decade

1. Victor Bockris, *Warhol* (New York: Da Capo Press, 1997), pp. 326–327.

2. Ibid., p. 335.

3. Bob Colacello, *Holy Terror: Andy Warhol Close Up* (New York: Harper Collins, 1990), p. 128.

4. Micahel Ferguson, *Little Joe, Superstar: The Films of Joe Dallesandro* (California: Companion Press, 1998), p. 109.

5. Bockris, p. 360–361.

6. Ibid., p. 361.

7. David Bourdon, *Warhol* (New York: Harry N. Abrams, Inc., 1989), p. 322.

8. Ibid., p. 243.

9. *Andy Warhol, Transcript of David Bailey's ATV Documentary* (London: Bailey Litchfield/Mathews Miller Dunbar Ltd., 1972).

10. Bockris, p. 370.

11. Ibid., p. 390.

12. Colacello, p. 308.

Chapter 7. The Final Years

1. Victor Bockris, *Warhol* (New York: Da Capo Press, 1997), p. 406.

2. Ibid., p. 426.

3. Hilton Kramer, "Art: Whitney shows Warhol Works," *The New York Times*, November 23, 1979.

4. Peter Schjeldahl, "Warhol and Class Content," *Art in America*, May, 1980.

5. Bob Colacello, *Holy Terror: Andy Warhol Close Up* (New York: Harper Collins, 1990), p. 423.

6. Eva Windmuller, "A Conversation with Andy Warhol," *Stern*, October 8, 1981.

7. Bockris, p. 445.

8. David Bourdon, *Warhol* (New York: Harry N. Abrams, Inc., 1989), p. 394.

9. Bockris, p 460.

10. Ibid., p. 461.

11. Bourdon, p. 392.

12. Bockris, p. 465.

13. John O'Connor and Benjamin Liu, *Unseen Warhol* (New York: Rizzoli, 1996), p. 17.

14. Bockris, p. 474.

15. Ibid., p. 477.

16. John Caldwell, *Carnegie Mellon Magazine*, 1986.

17. Thomas Sokolowski, Author's notes of speech in conjunction with *Warhol: Larger than Life* exhibit, MacKenzie Art Gallery, Regina, SK, February 29, 2008.

18. Paul Alexander, *Death and Disaster: The Rise of the Warhol Empire and the Race for Andy's Millions* (New York: Villard Books, 1994), p. 96.

19. Bockris, p. 494.

Chapter 8. The Andy Warhol Legacy

1. Paul Alexander, *Death and Disaster: The Rise of the Warhol Empire and the Race for Andy's Millions* (New York: Villard Books, 1994), p. 193.

2. Thomas Sokolowski, Author's notes of speech in conjunction with *Warhol: Larger than Life* exhibit, MacKenzie Art Gallery, Regina, SK, February 29, 2008.

3. Ibid.

4. David Bourdon, *Warhol* (New York: Harry N. Abrams, Inc., 1989), p. 418.

5. Ibid.

6. Ibid.

7. "The Andy Warhol Foundation: Past and Present," <http://www.warholfoundation.org/history.htm> (November 12, 2008).

8. Klaus Honnef, *Andy Warhol 1928-1987: Commerce into Art* (Koln, Germany: Benedikt Taschen Verlag, 1993), p. 93.

9. Eleanor Heartney, "The Religious Art of Andy Warhol.(Review)," *Art in America*, 1999, <http://www.highbeam.com/doc/1G1-54821847.html> (June 6, 2009).

10. Cliff Edwards, "The Religious Art of Andy Warhol," *Christian Century*, March 10, 1999, <http://findarticles.com/p/articles/mi_m1058/> (June 6, 2009).

11. Ibid.

12. David Bourdon, "Andy Warhol and the American Dream," *Andy Warhol: 1928-1987*, (Munich: Prestel-Verlag, 1993), p. 12.

13. Kerry A. Goodenow, "For His 80th, Warhol Granted More Than His 15 Minutes," *The Harvard Crimson* Online Edition, October 31, 2008, <http://www.thecrimson.com/article.aspx?ref=524996> (November 12, 2008).

14. Ibid.

15. Sokolowski.

Chronology

1. Matt Wrbican, "Andy Warhol Chronology," *The Warhol: Resources and Lessons*, 2006, <http://edu.warhol.org/20c_chron.html> (August 26, 2009).

Further Reading

Books

Demilly, Christian. *Pop Art*. Munich; New York: Prestel, 2007.

Greenberg, Jan and Sandra Jordan. *Andy Warhol: Prince of Pop*. New York: Delacorte Press, 2004.

Mason, Paul. *Pop Artists*. Chicago, Ill.: Heinemann Library, 2003.

Rubin, Susan Goldman. *Andy Warhol: Pop Art Painter*. New York: Abrams, 2006.

Spilsbury, Richard. *Pop Art*. Chicago, Ill.: Heinemann Library, 2008.

Internet Addresses

The Andy Warhol Foundation for the Visual Arts
<http://www.warholfoundation.org>

The Andy Warhol Museum
<http://www.warhol.org>

Index